CONTENTS

ANTHEM PUBLISHING

St. Basil the Great

The Fathers for English Readers

Richard Travers Smith
Vicar of St. Bartholomew's and Canon of St.
Patrick's, Dublin

ANTHEM PUBLISHING

St. Basil the Great

The Fathers for English Readers

Richard Travers Smith
Vicar of St. Bartholomew's and Canon of St. Patrick's, Dublin

ANTHEM PUBLISHING
Formatted and Printed in the United States of America,
Grand Rapids, MI, Under Whitmer's COVID tyranny.
A career politician is a career criminal.
Digital edition also available: https://amzn.to/2L3im4m
ISBN: 9798588085175

Editorial Preface

The editorial team at Anthem Publishing has determined that this book represents an important contribution to our knowledge of the Bible and Christian theology. For this reason, we have decided to reissue the book in an affordable paperback and eBook.

We believe that classic scholarship and classic works have a role to play in today's world. We believe classic scholarship can provide much needed perspective on the assumed superiority of modern scholars, and we believe classic treatises transcend the immediate wisdom of the modern world, imparting wisdom that, perhaps, has become unfashionable or difficult to accept.

Additionally, we believe this book as well as the others we publish are a critical part of our cultural identity. We hope that reissuing this book helps to preserve that identity while contributing to Christian theological discussion both today and in the future.

Thank you for purchasing this book from us. We do hope that the book's quality and design meet your standards and that you will find it edifying for many years to come.

—ANTHEM PUBLISHING

CHAPTER I
Early Life: Athens

St. Basil the Great was born about the year 329, of a Christian family, whose high religious character and sacrifices for the cause of truth had been for generations widely known in Asia Minor. It seems probable that the place of his birth was Cæsarea, in Cappadocia, the town of which he afterwards became bishop; but his father's connexions were more with Pontus than with Cappadocia, and some authorities place Basil's birth in the former province. He himself calls each of these countries in turn his native land.

Basil the elder—for father and son were named alike—was a teacher of rhetoric, and an advocate in large practice. He was a Christian of the best and most earnest type, and when Gregory of Nazianzus addressed his panegyric of the younger Basil to a large audience he was able to assume that the reputation of the father would be known to them all. But the future saint owed his earliest religious education to his grandmother Macrina, who brought him up with his brothers, and formed them upon the doctrine of the great Origenist and saint of Pontus, Gregory Thaumaturgus.

Macrina had not only been taught by the best Christian instructors, but had herself with her husband suffered for the faith. In the persecutions of Maximin she and her family were driven from their home and forced with a few companions to take refuge in a forest among the mountains of Pontus, where they spent nearly seven years, and were wont to attribute to the special interposition of God the supplies of food by which they were maintained at a distance from all civilization.

It must not be supposed that the charge of Basil's childhood thus committed to his grandmother indicated any deficiency in love or piety on the part of his mother. Her name was Emmelia, and Gregory describes her as fitly matched with her husband. They had ten children. Of the five sons three became bishops—Basil, Gregory of Nyssa, and Peter of Sebaste. The four youngest daughters were happily married, but Macrina, the eldest, devoted herself to the religious life, and exercised over Basil himself a most salutary influence at a very critical period in his career. In how great love and honour she was held by the whole family we know from the eulogium pronounced upon her by her younger brother, Gregory Nyssen.

Thus Basil was brought up under the most favourable circumstances as regards religion; nor was his education of a narrow type. He enjoyed from the instructions of his father, to which he passed while still a boy, very rich opportunities of classical culture, and his writings prove how willingly he profited by these, and by the university education to which they led, and how deeply he always valued them. We can, in fact, imagine few periods or places until we come to quite modern times which could have given to Basil's genius fairer development or wider exercise than did those which fell to his lot. But when we come to describe the condition of public affairs we must acknowledge that few periods could have prepared for him greater difficulties and disappointments. He was born four years after the orthodox faith had been formulated at the Council of Nicæa. His education and his own deepest tendencies of mind and soul responded to his early teaching in the Catholic belief. The slightest study of his works will convince us that it was no mere habit of profession which placed him among the defenders of the Nicene Creed, but a conviction so thorough that the slightest infringement of it would have been to him falsehood of the deepest dye.

For a mind so framed and furnished the times promised very badly. While Constantine lived Basil was but a boy; his youth and early manhood were passed under the reign of the Arian Constantius, to whom, after the brief episode of the reigns of Julian and Jovian, the Arian Valens succeeded in the dominion of the East. Thus for more than thirty years Arianism wielded the whole civil authority in the regions with which Basil was connected, save for a short three years, which were chiefly occupied by a heathen reaction, too weak and brief to do the truth the service of severe persecution. We have, perhaps, no right to complain that Arianism availed itself of the aid of the temporal power, seeing that the Catholics did the same when opportunity offered. Such, however, was the fact. The whole of Basil's mature life is to be passed under governments which will only vary from unfriendly opposition to actual persecution.

From the instructions of his father Basil passed to Cæsarea, a place of much literary eminence, where there were at the time excellent schools. Nazianzen, who

here, if not before, began to know him, informs us that
he gained the highest reputation even at that early
period, as well for intellectual eminence as for religious
character. He was a philosopher among philosophers,
an orator among orators, even before he had passed the
regular course in those branches of instruction; above
all, a priest among Christians so long before assuming
the order of the priesthood. Thus early did his wonderful
versatility impress observers.

The education which he received was altogether
Greek. There is the best reason to think that he did not
even know the Latin language. Certainly the classic
authors whom he quotes with so much appreciation are
uniformly Greek. The records which we have of the
education of his contemporary Julian assure us that it
was upon Homer and Hesiod, upon the great dramatists
of Athens and her historians and orators, that the
youthful genius of Basil was fed. Although Gregory
commends his Christian character at this period, the
custom of the age allows little doubt that he was still,
and for many years afterwards, unbaptized.

From Cæsarea he proceeded to Byzantium for further
improvement in learning. We know little of his progress
there, save that it was in Constantinople that he came in
contact with the great sophist Libanius, if indeed the
tradition of their intercourse and the letters which are
said to have afterwards passed between them are
genuine at all. In 351 Basil proceeded to Athens, the
step which in those days corresponded to entering a
university among ourselves. Of this part of his life we
have a full and very interesting record in the oration of
Gregory Nazianzen, who was at Athens some time
before his countryman's arrival, and had entered into
the spirit of the place with more enthusiasm than the less

imaginative Basil was at first able to feel.

Gregory informs us that Basil's reputation had preceded him to Athens, and that he was eagerly expected by many youths ready to compete for his friendship. It was the custom that the freshman should be received upon his first appearance with a torrent of jokes and banter, rough or refined according to his character, and designed, Gregory supposes, to take down his pride; he used then to be conducted in solemn procession to the bath, where the assembled youth were wont to burst into a horrible din of shouting, and beat at the doors in a frantic manner, to the great confusion of the raw lad whom they were conducting; from the bath he was escorted home with similar solemnity, and thenceforth considered to be free of the place. Basil alone, either because of his dignity of manner or the influence of his fellow-countryman, was spared the ordeal. But he did not entirely escape: for certain Armenian youths of senior standing got up a disputation with him, in which Gregory, not comprehending their insidious designs, was inclined at first to give aid to them rather than to Basil, who was already proving too strong for them. But presently perceiving the real state of the case, he threw his weight upon the side of his countryman, to the discomfiture of the assailants.

These circumstances drew the two Cappadocians together, and their acquaintanceship speedily deepened into the affection which, with one partial breach, was to last till death. They lived together, and aided one another in exhausting all the opportunities of learning which the place afforded. The discipline of university life at Athens was extremely lax. Town and gown riots not unfrequently took place, and contests between the pupils of rival teachers were very common. The pupils of different nations severally banded together and obnoxious authorities suffered severely at their hands; and misbehaviour, even at lecture, was often complained of. It was doubtless possible, as in other places, for an idle student to gain nothing whatever from the place, and for a diligent one to gain a great deal. The instruction was entirely professorial. The youths repaired to the house of their professor in the morning hours, attended sometimes by short-hand writers to take down his lecture. They brought with them their themes for correction, and they disputed in the presence of the teacher in order to train themselves for public speaking. When he spoke, they made no scruple of applauding; and the practice may surprise us less when we remember that the like was done by the congregations in the churches while listening to a sermon.[1] The chief teachers of Basil and Gregory were Proæresius, a Christian of Armenia, and Himerius of Bithynia, a heathen.

The two friends abstained wholly from the amusements which prevailed among the youth. Two paths alone, as Gregory informs us, were known to them,—that which led to the lecture-room of the teachers, and that which led to church. Gregory confesses what indeed we can well understand, that the heathen traditions of Athens and the magnificent remains of the fallen religion with which it was filled, brought no slight temptation to a young man's faith. But during the four years of Basil's sojourn no relaxation of his religious strictness took place; rather was it confirmed by resistance to the prevailing tone of his surroundings.

A frequent partner of their studies was Julian, the

---

[1] Capes. University Life in Athens, p. 110.

nephew of the reigning emperor Constantius. This
young prince was on very friendly terms with Basil, with
whom he was wont to read the Bible, and search out the
relation between its lessons and those of their heathen
teachers. Different indeed were the conclusions which in
after-life the two students were to draw from these
researches. Gregory declares himself to have disliked
and distrusted Julian from the first, on account of his
uneasiness, his self-consciousness, and his vanity.
Julian, however, caressed the two friends, and may have
seen in them, even at this time, possible instruments for
the reactionary designs which he was already planning.
He must have known that if they declined to serve him
for such a purpose, they were capable of becoming the
most formidable impediments to a restoration of
heathenism, as knowing the best it had to give, and yet
perfectly ready to go rejoicing to death in opposing it.

Gregory's account of the student life of his friend is
very glowing; and yet it is too well supported by the
results in Basil's after-years, and too similar to what has
been observed in the college days of other great men, to
allow us to call it an undiscriminating eulogy. He says
that Basil's industry and concentration were such that he
could have succeeded even without talent, and his
quickness of intellect such that he could have succeeded
without great labour. Uniting both he became so
brilliant a scholar that in each of many branches of study
he was as proficient as if he had studied it alone. His
favourite subjects were rhetoric,—which taught to speak
with force and fire, though in the use of this endowment
his ethical purpose was absolutely different from that of
the rhetoricians of the time; grammar,—which
"hellenized" his language to the most exquisite degree,
and taught him to observe the true style of history, the

canons of metre, and the laws of poetry; philosophy,—
that lofty science, in both its departments, the moral
speculation which has to do with human conduct, and
the dialectical which trains to argument. In this latter he
became so skilled that there was no escaping from the
force of his logic when he cared to use it. Astronomy,
geometry, and the science of numbers he studied only so
far as to be able to hold his own among those
acquainted with these branches of study. But in
medicine, which his own delicacy of health rendered
peculiarly interesting to him, he went so far as to acquire
the practice of the art. But all his intellectual eminence
was a small matter when compared with the purity of
his life.

Indeed the philosophy which Basil imbibed at
Athens, though not Christian, had the deepest
connexions with the morality of the Gospel. It was the
Neo-Platonic; and we know from the remains of Julian
what was its scope. It included three parts: logic, which
was called demonstrative, persuasive, or sophistic
according as it regarded the true, the probable, or the
apparent; physics which comprehended theology,
mathematics, and the theory of ideas; morals, or
practical philosophy, which was denominated ethics,
economics, or politics when applied respectively to the
direction of the individual, of the family, or of the State.
All this vast system formed a science of being, which
taught the mind of man first how to know and guide
itself and to find God within; secondly, to know God
and the world without; thirdly, to discern the end of
man and the means of attaining it.[2]

At last "the ship had been loaded with a cargo of

---

[2] Fialon. Saint Basile, p. 27.

learning," and the time arrived for Basil and Gregory to carry out the design long arranged between them of returning to their native land, there to pursue the religious life with greater strictness than was possible at Athens. The day of departure came, and with it the usual accompaniments, last words, seeing off the parting friend, attempts to retain him, lamentations, embraces, and tears. For there is nothing so sad in life, says Gregory, as for those who have been brought up together at Athens to be parted at once from each other and from her. Gregory suffered himself for the present to be prevailed on by the entreaties of fellow collegians and masters, who crowded round them to hinder their departure. But Basil, as we should expect, held by his purpose. He explained to his friends the causes of his departure, and left them very sadly; but he went, nor did Gregory remain long behind.

CHAPTER II
Cæsarea and Annesi: Ascetic Life

On Basil's return to Cæsarea (a.d. 355) the designs of religious life which he and his friend had formed at Athens appear to have been for a while forgotten amidst the admiration which his accomplishments excited in the world. His father was dead; his mother settled at Annesi, the place of his own early training, near to Neocæsarea. He practised rhetoric at Cæsarea with great success, and Neocæsarea contended for his presence. It has been inferred from a letter from Gregory, written to Basil at this period, that the strict morality of his life at Athens had given way, and that he was entangled in the pleasures of the world. It is hazardous to build such an impeachment upon the banter, probably rather exaggerated, of this letter. But we have the best reason for believing that Basil was at this period excessively vain and self-conceited. It is Gregory Nyssen, his brother, and devoted admirer as well, who is our authority for this statement. And the same truthful panegyrist relates to us the process of his cure. It was effected by his elder sister Macrina; she found him puffed up beyond measure with literary pride, despising all dignities, and looking down from his eminence upon those who held places of high worldly power. Macrina pressed him to embrace the life of a solitary, and at last succeeded in inducing him, like a new Moses, says his brother, to prefer the Hebrews to the treasures of Egypt.

At this period he was baptized, and shortly afterwards was ordained to the office of reader by Dianius, the bishop of Cæsarea, the revered friend of his youth. Gregory Nazianzen makes this incident in the life of his friend the text for a lamentation over the hasty ordinations of his time by which so many were introduced into the priesthood without due training in the minor offices that there was a danger lest the order most sacred of all should become the most ridiculous. Nobody, he says, is called a physician or a painter until he has learnt the nature of diseases or the mixing of colours and drawing of forms. But priests are manufactured off hand;—conceived and born simultaneously, like the giants in the fable. We make saints in a day, and bid men be holy and learned who have had no preparation and contribute nothing to the priesthood except a desire to enter it. Not so Basil, who was content to exercise the humble office of reading the Scriptures to the people long before he proceeded forward to the priesthood and episcopate.

He himself has given us in a letter, unwillingly written to Eustathius of Sebaste, an account of more than one disenchantment which he experienced at this period of his life.[3] He had spent, he confesses, many years in vanity, and had devoted a laborious youth to the wisdom of this world, which God has made foolish;

---

[3] Ep. ccxxiii.

expressions which we need not indeed accuse of the least exaggeration, but must balance by the remembrance of the constant use which the saint continued to make of his classical acquirements. At last, awaking as from a dream, he looked to the glorious light of the Gospel, and saw the uselessness of the wisdom of this world, which comes to nought. Lamenting his wretched life, he looked every way for some guidance to introduce him into the ways of piety. First he was eagerly desirous of making a change in his practical life long perturbed by intercourse with the wicked. "Therefore," he says, with a touching simplicity, "reading my Bible, and finding there that it is a great assistance to perfection that we should sell our goods and distribute to the poor brethren, and be entirely without care for the things of this life, and suffer our soul to be distracted by no affection towards things here, I wished to find some brother who had chosen this way of life, that with him I might pass the brief waves of this world." Repairing to Egypt, he found in Alexandria and other parts of that land, in Palestine, Cœle-Syria and Mesopotamia, many persons whose extraordinary abstinence, not only from food, but from sleep, whose constant labours and prayers moved his astonishment, since they treated their own flesh as if it was some strange residence in which they were sojourning. These holy men he deeply desired to imitate.

It was natural, then, that he should be greatly attracted by those who in his own country were already practising the ascetic life, and of whom Eustathius was the most eminent. In his simplicity, he thought their rough garments and girdles, and sandals of undressed hide, to be a sufficient proof of their genuine humility. And when others warned him, he would listen to nothing against the monks, but defended them against accusations of false doctrine. Experience undeceived him; and he found afterwards in these monks of the school of Eustathius (who was himself first a semi-Arian and afterwards a denier of the deity of the Spirit) opponents of his work, so turbulent and so deceitful, that a true account of their conduct must appear either incredible, or, if believed, a reason for hating the human race.

Now, the support of orthodoxy was an important part of the object for which Basil valued the ascetic life. There was the most urgent need of an organization for this purpose. The bishops and clergy of the time were, some of them, ignorant, and some deeply tainted with semi-Arianism. Even the best of them had made concessions in the things of faith to the difficulties of the time. Basil did not judge them hardly; his own revered old friend Dianius was of their number. But he chose a different course for himself, and proceeded to enlist a little army to fight the battle, whose whole life should be founded and organized upon Scriptural truth.

Great as was the wonder with which he viewed the solitary asceticism of Egypt and Palestine, the practical good sense of Basil revolted against a life whose end was centred in itself. His idea was to combine the ascetic life with the advantages of union and mutual aid. And he counted upon the assistance of his friend Gregory in carrying out this purpose. It was in the year 358 that Basil returned to Cæsarea, resolved to live a life in which absolute superiority to all indulgence should, instead of estranging him from refined enjoyment and the interests of his fellow men, aid him in the pursuit of both. In this design Gregory was pledged from the time of their college days to accompany him. But Gregory's

father, the bishop of Nazianzus, was old, and his son
unwilling to leave him. Basil appears, therefore, for a
short time to have followed his friend to Nazianzus; but
he soon abandoned this place for Annesi, the home of
his childhood, hard by the place where his mother and
sister were residing. What the method of his existence at
Annesi was we learn from the pressing letters in which
he urges Gregory to share his retreat. The idea of their
author is not to purchase heaven by the renunciation of
all earthly delights; on the contrary, the picture which
they present is designedly inviting to a man willing to
mortify the sensual desires. There was indeed but one
meal in the day and little sleep; manual labour, the
reading of Holy Scripture, prayer, conversation, and
psalmody, which imitated on earth the concert of the
angels, divided the day. But the description of the
natural beauties of the place which Basil lays before his
friend has ever been counted one of the most charming
specimens of his eloquence. Gregory was prevailed upon
to come, but found the life by no means equal to the
description, and very little to his taste. Never, he
declares, will he forget the soup and the bread, which his
poor teeth had much ado to pierce, and out of which
they had to drag themselves upwards as if getting out of
the mud. If Basil's good mother had not taken pity on
his hard case, he would no longer be in the land of the
living. And how can he omit to mention those gardens,
unworthy of the name, which grew no vegetables, and
for manuring which they had to cast out of the house
filth enough to have filled the Augean stable, or that
wagon which the two accomplished university men used
together to draw when they were levelling a hill,—
exertions which had left upon Gregory's poor hands
marks which they still bear? But this is not to be taken

too seriously. Gregory's succeeding letter expresses an eager longing to return to a life of such spiritual benefit.

The joint studies of Basil and Gregory were devoted to the sacred Scriptures, and it was at this period that they compiled the selection from the works of Origen which they called Philocalia. Origen was the most suggestive writer upon Bible subjects then accessible; certainly not the author who would have been chosen if the friends had been losing their intellectual vigour or spirit of free inquiry in a dull asceticism. But neither study nor prayer hindered Basil from evangelic labours. We learn from Gregory Nyssen that so many disciples congregated around him as to give his retreat the appearance of a town. And from thence he issued to conduct missions in Pontus and Cappadocia, rousing the indolent souls of a people little occupied with future hopes. He softened hard hearts, and brought many to repentance. He taught them to renounce the world, to form communities and build monasteries, to devote themselves to psalmody and preaching, to provide for the poor, constructing asylums for their accommodation, to take care of them when there, and to establish convents of women.[4] Thus he uplifted the ideal of the spiritual life through all the province. In a word, Basil commenced, during his retreat at Annesi the manysided work of religion and philanthropy, which he carried on as bishop to the last day of his life.

An episode in Basil's life, in which there was nothing to look back on with satisfaction, and which his enemies even made a reproach to him in after-days, was his visit to Constantinople with Basil of Ancyra, and Eustathius of Sebaste, to communicate the conclusions of the

------

[4] Ruffinus, quoted by Fialon, p. 48.

Council of Seleucia. In a council which followed at
Constantinople in the succeeding year, 360, the worldly
Acacius succeeded in carrying everything for the
cunningly veiled form of Semi-Arianism, which he
favoured at the time. Basil was afterwards accused by
Eunomius of cowardice in failing to oppose these
disastrous conclusions; but his subordinate position
probably deprived him of all power. And he retired from
Constantinople when the heretical creed of Ariminum
was presented by Constantius for signature. He
proceeded to Cæsarea, but the Arian emissaries
followed thither; and to his intense grief his bishop,
Dianius, was induced to sign the formula. Basil had
done his best to preserve the old man, for whom he
entertained the sincerest affection, from this step, too
much in harmony with the weak facility which had
always accompanied his gentleness. And when the deed
was done, Basil retired from Cæsarea to avoid the
painful step of making public that inability to
communicate with the bishop, to which the interests of
truth constrained him. But he afterwards disclaimed
with great energy the charge of having anathematized
the old man, who had but fallen into a snare, in which
well-nigh all the bishops of the East, including the elder
Gregory of Nazianzum, were caught. And when, two
years afterwards, amidst the troubles of Julian's heathen
reaction, Dianius felt his end approaching, he recalled to
his side the man upon whom his spirit leant for guidance, and died in Basil's arms, declaring with his last
breath that he had acted in the simplicity of his heart,
and never meant to cast doubt upon the creed of Nicæa,
with whose authors he desired to dwell in heaven. Such
were the difficulties which in those evil times overcame
all but the clearest and the most steadfast minds.

CHAPTER III
Life as a Presbyter at Cæsarea and Election to the Archbishopric

The death of Dianius occurred at a critical time. Julian was approaching; and the faithful of Cæsarea were greatly divided in their choice of a successor to the archbishopric. At the prompting of friendship, or from motives of piety, some proposed one candidate, some another. The election was finally carried by a popular impulse by no means without example in those days. Eusebius, one of the chief civil officials of the town, a man of high character but as yet unbaptized, was seized by the crowd, with the assistance of the soldiers, and hurried in spite of his own resistance to the bishops to be baptized and proclaimed elect. The bishops were forced to yield. But on the retirement of the crowd they desired to annul the election on the ground of violence. From this they were deterred by Gregory of Nazianzus the elder, who reminded them that in throwing doubt upon the election they were convicting themselves of cowardice.

Thus the choice of Eusebius stood; but this forcible transfer to the Church's service of a valuable civil official added to the irritation which Julian already felt toward Cæsarea for a tumult which had occurred there, and in which a temple of Fortune had been destroyed. The governor demanded of the bishops, under threat of the Emperor's wrath, the recall of the election. But Gregory answered firmly for his brethren that this was not one of the questions in which they could in conscience permit the civil power to interfere.

Basil was at Cæsarea during these transactions, and there is reason to believe that the course which things took may have been due to his influence. His birth and literary fame, increased at this time by the publication of his work against Eunomius, pointed him out as a leader, and himself a very probable selection for the vacant throne; and the monks were a compact and influential army of supporters to him. Thus it seems very likely that the choice of Eusebius was suggested by him. And, indeed, the decision with which the aged Gregory behaved was not much in harmony with his character, and makes it probable that he was prompted by a stronger will. Basil was incapable, it is true, of planning to set up a puppet for any selfish ends. But he had a nature capable of ruling, and the desire for rule which accompanies the capacity; and it is by no means impossible that he may have expected to be able to wield for the excellent ends which he had in view the authority of a bishop who, having no ecclesiastical experience, must be guided by some one.

And at first it seemed that such was to be the event Early in his episcopate, Eusebius ordained Basil to the priesthood. There was at that time a fashion, doubtless a reaction of the higher minds against the eager and hasty ordinations which were so common, but sometimes partaking of affectation, to accept orders only upon compulsion. Such had been the case in Eusebius's own consecration. Gregory of Nazianzus had shortly before been ordained a priest in the same way, and now Basil was made a presbyter by force, and his whole time became so occupied with preaching and with business as to leave him no leisure even to write to his friends. It is not surprising that the bishop should have become jealous. He was a good man and a brave one, but by no means accustomed to see himself eclipsed. And his behaviour to Basil became exceedingly offensive. Whether a taint of pride in the presbyter may have had its share in producing the misunderstanding we know not, but his conduct when it had arisen was admirable. Many circumstances combined to render it perfectly easy for him to have made a schism. The party of Eusebius was discredited on account of his tumultuous election; the character of Basil was enthusiastically reverenced, and the more pious party of the city was on his side; and lastly, there were present at the time some Western bishops perfectly ready to consecrate him at a sign. Many a man would have yielded to the temptation, for indeed the election of Eusebius was not above just suspicion. But Basil resisted, and withdrew at the advice of Gregory to the Pontic retreat, whither his friend accompanied him; and the succeeding period was spent in study and in the rule and direction of the great monastic and mission work already on foot.

A part of the care of the two friends was devoted to the composition of works against Julian, whose Hellenic reaction took place at this period. That prince, on coming to the throne, had proceeded to set on foot the restoration of heathenism, on which his mind had been set ever since his Athenian days, and he fixed his eye upon his Cappadocian college friends as fit instruments in such a work. They certainly were richly equipped by knowledge of both heathen and Christian literature, for the part of learned foes to the faith, had conviction not stood in the way, just as we might easily imagine Julian himself, had not the mistakes of an education conducted by unworthy Christians prejudiced him against the faith, taking his proper place by the side of his old acquaintances in the great cause of culture with self-denial. The fact of Julian's advances to Basil and his friend we know from the writings of Gregory against him. But of the correspondence between Julian and Basil, contained among the letters of the latter, all is doubtful, and part almost certainly spurious.[5] And after the catastrophe of Julian, Basil observed towards his memory a dignified silence, which is certainly more attractive than the vehement and exultant reproaches heaped on it by Gregory.

The threat of a new persecution recalled Basil to Cæsarea. Valens had, after the short reign of Jovian, succeeded to the throne of Constantinople. He is said to have possessed the merit of simplicity of life, and to have imposed some check on the waste of the court. But his elevation was not due to personal qualities, but to the favour of his brother Valentinian. The latter prince established religious toleration in the West; but Valens, baptized by the Arian Eudoxius, patriarch of Constantinople, fell into the hands of that party, and lent them the whole influence of the empire for the advancement of their belief. His own character, in spite of the fact that he had kept his faith under Julian, was

---

[5] *See* Garnier, Vita S. Bas., cap. viii. Fialon, p. 155.

very weak. In the words of Gibbon, "he derived his
virtues as well as his vices from a feeble understanding
and a pusillanimous temper"; and the contemptuous
excuse of the same historian, that the ecclesiastical
ministers of Valens may have exceeded the orders or
even the intentions of their master, is probably true. But
from the second year of his reign we find him traversing
the East with a band of Arian courtiers, reducing the
orthodox everywhere to subjection.

Gregory gives a sombre picture of the consternation
which this invasion of heretics diffused. It was a
hailstorm roaring frightfully and crushing all the
churches upon which it fell; an emperor loving gold and
hating Christ; who arose after the apostate Julian, not
indeed himself an apostate, but none the kinder for that
reason to the orthodox, who declined "to weigh duty as
in a balance, and to separate the one and indivisible
nature in itself, and to cure the impious restrictions of
Sabellius by a more impious diffusion and
dismemberment." Eusebius felt himself unequal to the
encounter, and invited to his aid Gregory of Nazianzus,
the only ecclesiastic whom he thought able to supply the
place of the man whom he had driven from his side. But
Gregory, as might be anticipated, was entirely
indisposed to accept advances at the expense of his
friend. "To honour me," he said, "while you insult him,
is to caress me with one hand and strike me with the
other. Believe me, if you treat him as he merits, the
credit will return to yourself, and I shall come after him
as the shadow after the body." At first the bishop was
offended by this frankness; but at last he softened, and
an interview with Gregory took place, which formed the
basis of a successful mediation on the part of the latter.
Basil, he informs us, was very easily prevailed upon. He

admitted at once that the time was not one for
maintaining a private grudge, and returned to Cæsarea.
Probably both Eusebius and he had derived valuable
lessons from what had occurred: the former had seen his
own need of support, and the latter had learnt prudence
in the exercise of his influence. Certain it is that from
this time forward the whole rule of the diocese fell into
the hands of the presbyter, without any further symptom
of jealousy in the bishop. Basil was his counsellor upon
all occasions, but made it his first care to honour the
prelate before his flock. If there was any instinct of a
courtier in this, it was exercised for ends that were
perfectly pure and true.

During the years that Basil exercised authority under
the name of Eusebius he effected a vast amount of good.
To preaching and the charge of a parish were added a
multitude of other cares: the maintenance of the rights
of the Church against the civil magistrates; the
reconciliation of differences; the succour of those who
were in need, always with spiritual aids, often also with
temporal; the support of the poor; the entertainment of
strangers; the care of virgins; monastic rules, delivered
by writing or by word of mouth; arrangement of the
prayers;[6] decoration of the sanctuary. Finally, when, in
370, a terrible famine occurred, especially severe in
Cappadocia on account of its distance from the sea,
Basil crowned his services by preserving the lives of a
great number of people. He devoted to this purpose the
whole remains of his property, long since, indeed,
unused for his personal wants, but subject still to his
control, and the gifts which, by the most fervid appeals,
he was able to extract from the rich.

---

[6] This expression of Gregory has been held to point to Basil's compilation of the
Liturgy which bears his name.

In the same year, 370, Eusebius died, and Basil received his last breath, as he had that of his predecessor. It will be readily conceived that Basil was pointed out for successor by the voice of the best people in the town, of the clergy and monks; but the opposition was very strong, including, as it did, the bishops of the province, the civil magistrates, the rich, who revolted against his unceasing claims of charity, and the loose livers of the place. According to the canons, the bishops of the province were to assemble on the vacancy of a see and appoint a successor by the suffrages of the clergy and people. But in point of fact their hands were constantly forced by the influence of the rich and the tumultuous cries of the populace. Thus a severe contest was to be faced; and Basil was convinced, probably with perfect correctness, that the cause of genuine religion depended upon his election. It was natural that he should desire the assistance of his friend; but he knew the fastidious temper of Gregory, and took the doubtful step of feigning sickness as the ground for the summons. His state of health was, indeed, never so strong as to deprive such a statement of some colour; but the pretence failed of its effect, for Gregory met the bishops assembling, and, guessing the condition of things, returned hastily to Nazianzus, whence he wrote to reproach Basil and to advise retirement from the city during the election. But the bishop, his father, took a more practical view of the necessities of the case. And at his prompting, his son, though still unwilling to repair to Cæsarea himself, wrote to that church in favour of his friend, and (a still more effectual measure) sent for Eusebius of Samosata, the most eminent bishop of the country. Eusebius, in spite of the wintry season, made haste to the scene of action, where his weight decided in favour of Basil all parties except the bishops. The bishops tried every device to escape; they wrote to Bishop Gregory suggesting that he need not trouble himself to come. They maintained that while Basil's claims to elevation could not be denied, his health was unequal to the duties of the episcopate. And finally, when they were obliged to yield, only two of them were found willing to join in the consecration. Now the canons required three. But if, as seems to have been the case, it was hoped in this way to nullify the election, the plan was disappointed. For the aged Gregory of Nazianzus, though scarce able to stand, had himself lifted from his bed and carried in a litter to Cæsarea, where he presided over the election and consecration of the new bishop, and returned home restored, as his son informs us, to the strength of youth by the good work in which he had been engaged. The election was heard of at the court of Constantinople as a severe check; but the orthodox churches everywhere received the news with exultation, and Athanasius of Alexandria made it matter of special thanksgiving to God that a bishop should have been given to Cappadocia such as every province might wish for itself.

CHAPTER IV
Archbishop of Cæsarea and Theologian

The position in which Basil was placed by this election was magnificent if the reality of power had accompanied the name. He was Archbishop of Cæsarea, Metropolitan of Cappadocia, and Exarch of the diocese of Pontus. In the latter character his jurisdiction extended over half Asia Minor, but the authority was very indefinite. The exarchate was weakened by the institution of metropolitans, and was on the way to be absorbed in the patriarchate of Constantinople. His position as archbishop and metropolitan of Cappadocia was scarcely more satisfactory. For the suffragans who had refused to take part in his election continued their insubordination; and, wonderful to say, an uncle of Basil was among the malcontents. The difference was aggravated by a silly attempt at reconciliation devised by Gregory (Nyssen) Basil's younger brother. He was a very loyal soul, but not very wise; a comparison of his panegyric on his great brother with that of Gregory Nazianzen suffices to show alike his affection and his

poverty of mind. And upon this occasion he conceived
the notable plan of writing a letter to Basil in the name
of his uncle; the well-intended forgery was of course at
once discovered. But in about a year the breach was
closed by a kindly and submissive letter from Basil
himself to his uncle, little consistent with the pride
which is attributed to him. And it was followed by a
reconciliation on the part of the other bishops, both with
Basil and the elder Gregory, who bad taken so vigorous
a part in the election. There is reason, however, to think
that this submission of the bishops was merely a
measure to which they were driven by the public
opinion of the religious people and the monks among
their flocks, and implied very little cordial co-operation.

Towards the close of 371 a terrible blow was inflicted
upon the city of Cæsarea. The province of Cappadocia
was divided into two, and this measure of
administration deposed Cæsarea from its position and
transferred some of the most valuable portions of its
society to Podandum, where the capital of the separated
part of the province was fixed. Basil in vain attempted
by urgent letters to persons of influence to hinder this
dismemberment; all that could be obtained was the
transference of the new capital to Tyana. And this State
measure brought troubles to the Church of a wholly
unexpected kind. For Anthimus, bishop of Tyana,
insisted that an ecclesiastical separation followed the
secular, and claimed rank as metropolitan. Some of the
bishops of the province were too ready to aid him in this
revolt, and he proceeded to seize on revenues which
properly belonged to the church of Cæsarea.

This would have been of itself enough; but the same
circumstances led, by a perverse combination of events,
to the only serious wound which the friendship of Basil

and Gregory received throughout their lives. Gregory,
had with his usual extreme delicacy declined to join his
friend on his first appointment to the archbishopric, lest
interested motives should be imputed. But on the news
of the troubles arising from the division of the province,
he offered his presence, and came to Cæsarea, where
Basil had to contend with preposterous charges of
heresy brought against him by the friends of Anthimus.
And when Basil found it necessary to proceed to the
scene of action, Gregory accompanied him, and
displayed no small courage in an encounter of physical
force with the party of Anthimus, who intercepted
certain revenues which Basil was in person conducting
through a pass of Mount Taurus.

It may have been on this very occasion that the
design suggested itself to Basil of erecting a bishopric at
Sasima, and appointing to it his accomplished and
martial friend. Sasima was an important situation at a
junction of roads, and very well situated for looking
after these contested revenues: but it was, if we may
believe Gregory himself, a detestable place, filled with
dust, noise, and travellers, without natural charm and
without society. To this uninviting see Basil, after
consultation with the elder Gregory, consecrated the
brilliant son in his own despite. We can perfectly
understand his motives. He entertained for himself the
severest views of obedience to duty, and did not
sufficiently reflect that to choose unpleasant duties is
one thing, and to be entrapped or forced into them is
quite another.

The act was doubtless an error. Gregory submitted,
and after some delay was induced chiefly by an
injudicious attempt of Anthimus to tamper with his
loyalty) to do his best for his poor diocese. But he

complained violently, and while retaining the deepest reverence and love for Basil, was never able to think of this passage save as a blot upon the consistency of his friendship. The forced union with this unattractive bride proved so great a difficulty in Gregory's way when he was called to the splendid post of patriarch of Constantinople that his expulsion is partly attributed to it. And after all, the purpose with which Basil had appointed him does not seem to have been effected. For Anthimus so far gained his point that the second Cappadocia received an independent jurisdiction, though the terms of the arrangement are obscure. However, in estimating the blame to be assigned to Basil for his error and the amount of real offence which his act gave to his friend, we must remember that it was a fashion of the time for the clergy to be forcibly ordained to posts; that Gregory's style is very apt to exaggerate; that the consent of his father had been given to his consecration, and that not merely did Gregory eulogize his friend shortly after his death, but maintained the kindliest intercourse with him in life long after this unfortunate affair.

In spite of disappointments and defeats Basil bore bravely up. If his bishops opposed him, he multiplied sees and appointed to them men after his mind. His clergy, from having been an unsettled and sometimes an immoral class, became a devoted band, not only working hard at their vocation, but supporting themselves by the labour of their own hands; so well reputed in the East that bishops sent to Basil for priests whom they might nominate as their successors; so fixed to their work that presently it was hard for their bishop himself to find a man sufficiently unemployed to carry a letter for him. And his charitable institutions developed

themselves on a scale large enough to attract the
jealousy of the civil power. At Cæsarea arose a kind of
small town, including hospitals, asylums for strangers,
and all that apparatus of aid for misery which the State
ought to have furnished, but did not; all built by the
money which Basil's eloquence and example drew from
the rich; all served by his monks, among whom he
himself chose the most trying labour of all—the care of
the lepers.

Basil's relations to the temporal power were summed
up and exemplified in one celebrated passage of his life.
It formed one of the earliest scenes of a contest which
has since often recurred, not with the State as heathen
and persecuting like that of the early centuries, but with
the State as Christian, inflicting no wounds, making no
martyrs, yet demanding that the Church should accept
from it the measure of the truth which she is to preach.
It was in 372 that the approach of Valens to Cæsarea
was heralded by an advanced guard of courtiers to make
ready the submission of the Catholics for their master.
Two of these ecclesiastical negotiators are known to us:
Modestus, the prætorian prefect, a worthy who had
advanced to power under Constantius by detective
services of a discreditable kind, and had sacrificed to
idols under Julian; and Demosthenes, the prefect of the
kitchen, one of those wretched eunuchs of the court
whose insolence stirred the contempt alike of Basil and
of Gregory. The details of the archbishop's interview
with Modestus are given in somewhat different forms,
and have plainly received a dramatic colouring. Some of
Basil's answers have brought on him the charge of pride;
for instance, to the prefect's exclamation, "Never has
any one spoken to me in such a tone," Basil is said to
have answered, "That is because you have never before

met a true bishop." What is certain is, that an interview took place in which Basil's courage and the impossibility of frightening by threats of fine a man who possessed no property, or by threats of corporal punishment a man who cared nothing for life, reduced the prefect to discomfiture.

Valens followed, but his first act placed him at a hopeless disadvantage. There never was a monarch whose person required more of the assistance which splendid surroundings and crowds of courtiers impart; for he was small of stature, dark of complexion, disfigured by a pearl on the eye, excessively timid, and very ill acquainted with Greek. Basil, on the other hand, though penniless through his own act, was ever a gentleman in manner and appearance as he was by birth. He was tall in stature, very emaciated, with a massive brow and piercing eye. He was more than a match for Valens even in the midst of his court, yet the Emperor placed himself in a position in which all impressive surroundings were transferred to the advantage of his opponent. He attended service in the great church of Cæsarea on the feast of the Epiphany. There was a sea of worshippers, who chanted the psalms with a sound like thunder, and the archbishop erect behind the altar, as was the custom of the time, celebrated the divine mysteries with his clergy ranged in long array on each side. The Emperor was prepared with an offering, but none advanced to take it, no one knowing whether Basil would present it from heretical hands. The archbishop seeing that the poor man was on the point of fainting under the impressions of the scene, himself came forward to receive the offering.

An interview afterwards took place behind the veil of the sanctuary, in which, if we may trust Theodoret, the

archbishop discussed with the Emperor on equal terms
the great questions of theology; and the great man was,
as sometimes happens, put in good humour by a quip
upon one of his own dependents. For the prefect of the
kitchen interposing in the discussion, committed a gross
vulgarism in language, upon which the archbishop
observed that we had here a Demosthenes who could
not speak Greek, and had better return to his sauces.
The Emperor returned well pleased with the interview,
and made a grant to Basil of land for his establishments
of charity. But soon the Arian party resumed their
empire over his feeble mind, and he signed the decree
for Basil's exile. The saint required no long preparation,
having no baggage to bring but his writing-tablets, and
he was on the point of departure when he was
summoned to the palace to pray over Galatius, the son
of the Emperor, who had been seized with sudden
illness, which the fears of his mother ascribed to divine
vengeance for the treatment which the archbishop had
received. Basil made it a condition of his prayers that the
boy should be baptized in the Catholic faith. And the
child for the time recovered; but was baptized by the
Arians, and shortly afterwards died. Whether or not a
miracle interposed to prevent the signing of a new
decree of exile, or that the father found it impossible to
persecute the man who had prayed by his dying child,
Valens departed without further demands. And from
this time forward Basil was on terms, if not of cordiality,
yet generally of peace with the civil powers, Arian as
they were. When his protection disappointed the
interested designs of an official who desired to marry a
young widow against her will, and the Vicar of Pontus
threw the weight of his authority on the side of his
subordinate, a popular tumult arose, in which men,

women, and children took part, and the obnoxious
governor would have been torn in pieces but for Basil's
interposition. Modestus has now become his very good
friend, whom he compliments in Eastern style when
asking some favour for the distressed. And many others
in high places are willing to render similar service. More
than all, he actually proceeds to restore the episcopate of
Armenia armed with the authority of Valens himself.
But disappointment met him in the Church, in
comparison to which the hostility of the State was a
light matter. One bishop with whom he had to deal may
be truly called his evil genius. Eustathius of Sebaste was
not indeed in the grosser sense a worldly man. It was
not for the sake of temporal enjoyments that he accepted
and rejected so many creeds; but he was possessed with
an incurable inconstancy or carelessness about truth,
which made his ascetic life a mere means of deception.
Basil's connection with Eustathius brought upon him
rude treatment from the much-respected but narrow-
minded Theodotus of Nicopolis, who was followed by
many of the orthodox; and having thus damaged the
reputation of the archbishop by his friendship,
Eustathius proceeded to damage it further by his enmity.
It might seem almost incredible that such a man should
be able to bring Basil under a suspicion of heterodoxy.
But so it was: a letter innocently written by him to
Apollinaris twenty-five years before, was raked up, and
he was accused of complicity with the heresy of that
teacher; certain expressions used, perhaps incautiously,
by Basil in the public prayers, were tortured into proofs
of unsoundness upon the doctrine of the Holy Ghost
Even his friend Gregory seemed shaken in his
confidence by a vehement attack on Basil's orthodoxy
by an old monk at a festival. The Church of Neocæsarea

itself, the home of his childhood, was entirely alienated from him. And we realize, for the encouragement of all who in after-times have to contend for the truth, that it was not only by the heterodox or the careless that this great saint was denounced, but by the ultra orthodox and the religious world as well. No doubt he had many friends to stand by him in his battle. But here, also, he was sorely maimed by the exile of Eusebius of Samosata. And when in his loneliness he turned for aid to the bishops of the West, his repeated and touching appeals for succour and sympathy brought no response whatever. It is true that in 375 a synod was held in Illyria, and addressed to the East an energetic letter, which we still possess, in opposition to the chief errors of the times. And the Emperor Valentinian accompanied it by an epistle to the bishops of Asia, in which he directs that the Nicene doctrine shall be everywhere taught. No one, it is added, can be allowed to plead that he is following the faith of his Emperor (Valens); for this were to forget the Scripture principle, "Render unto Cæsar the things which are Cæsar's, and to God the things which are God's." It is characteristic of the position of Valens in the empire, and of the amount of his personal weight, that his own name appears attached to this document, so directly levelled against his opinions and influence. But the death of Valentinian in the same year caused these efforts for the assistance of the hard-pressed Eastern Catholics to fall still-born; and the civil powers with whom Basil was in contact remained favourers of Arianism until his life was so near its close that, like our own Hammond, he scarcely witnessed the reaction. It was in August 378 that Valens perished miserably in the rout of Hadrianople; and on the 1st of January succeeding Basil expired at Cæsarea, worn out at the age of fifty. His last words were those of so many saints before and since: "Into Thy hands I commend my spirit."

Like many other great workers, Basil seems himself never to have known how much he had done. After his death every one started forward to praise. The crowd of people of all classes and religions at his funeral was so great that many were crushed to death in the attempt to touch the bier, or catch a glimpse of his form. And seventy years after his death the General Council of Chalcedon called him the greatest of the fathers.

The extant works of St. Basil, as they stand arranged in the Benedictine edition, are as follow:—

I. Nine Homilies entitled Hexaemeron, being a series of Sermons upon the Six Days Creation. Homilies upon Psalms i., vii., xiv., xxviii., xxix., xxxii., xxxiii, xliv., xlv., xlviii., lix., lxi, cxiv. Five Books against Eunomius the Anomæan; the last two of which are supposed by some to be from another hand. A Commentary on the first sixteen chapters of Isaiah, which, if it be Basil's, as the weight of authority supposes, is a work of the earlier years of his ministry.

II. Homilies upon Fasting (2); upon the text "Take heed to thyself"; upon Thanksgiving; upon the Martyr Julitta; upon the text, "I will pull down My Barns and Build Greater"; to the Rich; upon the Famine; that God is not the Author of Evil; to the Angry; on Envy; on the beginning of the Book of Proverbs; on Holy Baptism; to Drunkards; on The Faith; on the text, "In the beginning was the Word"; on the Martyr Barlaam; on the Martyr Gordius; on the Forty Holy Martyrs; on Humility; that we must not cling to earthly things; on a fire which had happened near the church; to Young Men on reading the Heathen Literature; on the Martyr Mamas; against the Sabellians.

The ascetic works comprise the Ethica, or Scriptural
Rules of Morality; the Monastic Rules at large; the
Rules more briefly treated; the Rules of Penance for
Monks; the Monastic Constitutions. The two books on
Baptism are apparently proved by the Benedictine editor
not to be Basil's.

III. A work upon the Holy Spirit, in thirty chapters;
365 Letters, a few of which are certainly spurious. A
Treatise on True Virginity, considered spurious by the
Benedictine editor.

Lastly, we must not omit the Liturgy of St. Basil,
extant under two forms, in Greek and Coptic. There is
no good reason for refusing to believe in the genuineness
of this work; for a great agreement existed in the
testimony of antiquity to the fact that Basil composed a
liturgy. The extant Greek probably represents it in all
essential features. It is still used during a portion of the
year in the Orthodox Eastern Church.

CHAPTER V
Personal Traits

We shall commence our examination of these works by endeavouring to gather from them some personal traits which may help us better to know the man. It has been alleged by his detractors that his bosom fault was pride; even friends have admitted that there was ground for the charge, and he was accused of it in his lifetime,[7] though as he thinks very unjustly. The charge may have been, however, in some sense true, but it must be observed that one of the principal pieces of evidence for this defect is almost certainly imaginary. It consists of a passage in the Chronicon of Jerome, which all the MSS. but one refer, not to Basil at all, but to Photinus, the mention of whom stands in the preceding sentence.[8] Vossius, for the purpose of depreciating Jerome as a detractor, eagerly adopted the reading which refers the words to Basil, and Gibbon grasped at it in order to sneer at the Church for concealment of Basil's defects. But there is little doubt that Jerome never applied the

---

[7] Ep. ccxxiv.
[8] *See* Vallarsi on S. Jerome *in loc*.

description to him at all. Gregory Nazianzen repels the charge by alleging Basil's care for the sick and poor, an answer which would be indeed very insufficient if it referred to mere passing acts of humiliation, such as the Papal washing of poor men's feet. But it will, perhaps, be considered that the persistent and long-continued work of a bishop in personal attendance on the most repulsive diseases in an hospital is no such very bad reply to the charge of pride.

If Basil was naturally of a proud spirit, as perhaps he was, he deserves the praise of having forced himself to face the humiliations which his ceaseless struggles for orthodoxy brought upon him. He might have intrenched himself in his diocese, where his popularity was so great, and persuaded himself that it was not his business to interfere with the rest of the East, or that there was nothing which he could do. This is the species of pride which he had to complain of in the bishops of the West. He certainly did not display it himself. Nor when he is insulted and repelled either by heretics, or, as sometimes happened, by orthodox fanatics, does he either preserve the silence or display the resentment of a proud spirit. As for his treatment of the vulgar courtiers of Valens, it is very difficult to blame him for the contempt he displayed towards them. It was not merely an ebullition of natural temperament, but the most truthful tone which he could have taken, and by far the most wholesome for them: there is a time for all things, and this was what that time required. He slighted them at the time of their power and his weakness; but there is no record of his ever behaving in like fashion to any one who was poor, or in need of his aid. While, then, we do not deny that pride may have been natural to Basil, we cannot allow it to have assumed the proportions of a vicious habit: rather it was used for good, with only such taint of defect remaining as necessarily belongs to human nature.

One passage in Basil's life has caused this charge to be entertained by some churchmen otherwise well disposed to admire him: his relations to Pope Damasus. There is no doubt a singular absence in Basil of that "dropping-down deadness" of manner (if we may borrow Sydney Smith's phrase), which the bishops of Rome have been accustomed to demand. It is, of course, futile to accuse him of pride for the non-recognition of claims on the part of the Pope, which it never entered Basil's mind to conceive, but there is no doubt that he shows himself unwilling to concede even that degree of submissiveness which the bishops of Rome at that time thought their due. The reason is to be found in the careless and even heartless neglect with which he conceived the troubles of the East to have been treated by the Western bishops living at ease. Some writers, recognizing the absence of early evidence for the papacy, have seen a proof of the hand of Providence upon it in the constant readiness of the popes to give at every emergency the aid that was required of them. Certainly the treatment of Basil's appeals to the West is no mean proof to the contrary. A great opportunity was here missed, and a distinctly anti-papal character was impressed upon the writings of that father, whom, perhaps beyond all others, the East reveres. It should be also remarked, however, that the adoption of an independent tone towards Rome was a kind of tradition in the see of Cæsarea. S. Firmilian, whose letter to S. Cyprian in relation to the controversy about re-baptism has been ever a great stumbling-block to the supporters of the Papacy, was, at an interval of a century, Basil's

predecessor as bishop at Cæsarea, and the latter calls
him "our Firmilian."

If Basil displayed any pride towards men, he
certainly did not allow it to intrude into his relations to
God. It may seem strange to some that an ascetic and a
follower after perfection should show a deep sense of
sin; but so it is. He is thoroughly sincere when he
declares that he is so far from claiming to be sinless that
he knows his life to be full of innumerable faults, and
pours forth continual tears for his sins, if perchance he
may obtain favour of God,[9] or when he attributes his
misfortunes to his sins. "Pray," he begs his friend, "for
my miserable life, that, freed from these temptations, I
may begin to serve God."[10]

But he is very sensitive to desertion and unkindness.
He cannot think, though he broods over it constantly,
why such things should be believed against him.[11] He
knows that nothing is more hated among the religious
people of the time than his name. Those who take the
middle course, as they think, and setting out from the
same principles as he, decline to follow them to their
logical conclusions, because these are hateful to the ears
of the populace; these "moderate" persons are all
against him. How can he but feel it? His only comfort
lies in his bodily infirmity, which assures him that he
will not live long,[12] and when he recovers for a time, he
is sorry for it, knowing the evils to which he returns.[13]
May God give you, he prays, the blessings of Jerusalem
above, because you did not believe falsehoods about

---

[9] Ep. cciv.
[10] Ep. ccxlix.
[11] Ep. cxxxi.
[12] Ep. ccxii.
[13] Ep. ccli.

me.[14]

The fault which we should consider most obvious in Basil's letters is despondency and readiness to complain, due, probably, to the disease of the liver with which he had to contend all his life through. No doubt his low spirits make the indomitable energy more remarkable, which never allowed his work to grow slack through despair. But knowing what we do of the effect which that work had, both in his own diocese and in the churches of the East, it seems strange that he should say, "I seem to myself for my sins to succeed in nothing."[15]

His health was, indeed, wretched all his life through, "from his earliest youth."[16] When in health, he was weaker than other people when their recovery is despaired of.[17] In sickness he complains that his body has failed him altogether. Fifty days has he been sick of a fever, which not finding material enough in his poor body to nourish it, remained in his dried-up flesh as in a burnt-out wick, and wore him out utterly. And then his old plague of the liver coming in besides, deprived him of food, deprived him of sleep, and kept him on the borders of life and death, allowing him only just enough of life to feel his pains.[18] He is reduced to the condition of being actually thinner than himself,[19] and is only so far alive that he breathes.[20] And even when he has grown a little better, he remains so weak that the exertion of visiting the Church of the Martyrs in a carriage throws him back nearly into the same condition

---

[14] Ep. ccxliv.
[15] Ep. cclxvi.
[16] Ep. cciii.
[17] Ep. cxxxvi.
[18] Epp. c. and ccxxxviii.
[19] Ep. cxciii.
[20] Ep. cxcvi.

again.[21] After a journey into Pontus he is afflicted with intolerable sickness; but in the midst of all this he is taking care for the churches of Lycia, and making out a list of well-disposed persons in that quarter with whom a representative of orthodoxy, if sent into the country, is to place himself in communication.

Basil, if proud, was certainly not independent of love; the practice of asceticism had not the result of deadening his affections. Although his monastic rule demands so much renunciation of the ties of blood, yet he laments for his mother as "his only comfort in life," and in the alienation from his uncle (for which he was not to blame) he shows the strongest repugnance to disputes among relations.[22] "Honoured brother," he writes to a friendly bishop, "we feel an exceeding hunger for love.[23]" "We want brothers more than one hand wants the other."[24] He declares that the reception of a letter from a friend is to him like water to a tired racehorse.[25] He entertains a most affectionate remembrance of those who had been kind to him in youth. Thus he repels, with the utmost vehemence, the charge of having anathematized "the most blessed Dianius." Rather is he conscious of having been brought up from his earliest years in love for Dianius, and been accustomed to reverence his venerable priestly air, and as he grew older to delight in his company, for his simplicity, and nobleness, and freedom of manners, his magnanimity and mildness, together with his good temper, his gaiety and accessibility, combined with dignity.[26] A

---

[21] Ep. ccii.

[22] Epp. xxx. and lx.

[23] Ep. xci.

[24] Ep. xcvii.

[25] Ep. ccxxii.

[26] Ep. li.

corresponding affection Basil felt for Neocæsarea, the place to which he was accustomed from his boyhood, where he was brought up by his grandmother.[27] How dearly would he love to see his friend Eusebius and return with him in memory to boyhood, when they had the same home, and fireside, and teacher, the same amusements and studies, and pleasures, and wants. If he could but meet his friend, he might brush away this weight of age and seem young instead of old.[28] And his love for the friends of his own youth naturally drew with it that love for young people which is so attractive in the old. He has had with him the two sons of a friend for a festival day, and sends back "our" sons safe to their father, telling him that their love of God has helped him to spend the holy day in a perfect manner, and praying to the God who loves mankind that the angel of peace may be given them for a helper and companion of their way.[29] And when the two sons of Olympius have brought him letters from their father, they so comfort his afflicted soul that he forgets the poison which his enemies are scattering to his injury.[30] A like delight he expresses in Icelium, the daughter of his friend Magninianus.[31] He is assured that a rich reward must wait the father from the Lord for such an education of his children. And his affection for Gregory of Nazianzus, during boyhood, youth, and mature age, may be called one of the celebrated friendships of the world. It was one of the great moulding facts of life for both of them.

---

[27] Ep. ccx.

[28] Ep. xi.

[29] Ep. cclxxi.

[30] Ep. ccxi.

[31] Ep. cccxxv.

He knew, of course, what it was to find a friend
capricious or mistrustful, or to lose him amidst the sad
disputes of the times. If you remain in our communion,
he says to such a one, this were the best thing that could
happen, and worth the most earnest prayer. If others,
however, have drawn thee to them, that were sad
indeed, for why should not the loss of such a brother be
so? but if I have no other consolation, I have at least, by
the instrumentality of the same persons, been well
exercised in such losses.[32] To him it seems that one who
thinks of casting off a friend should first reflect long and
anxiously, spend many a sleepless night, and seek, with
many tears, God's guidance to the truth.[33] But when
calumny attempts to injure him with his friend, he can
write that the caluminator injures three persons,—the
subject of his slander, and the person to whom it is
addressed, and himself. Of the injury done to himself as
the subject he will say nothing; his friend knows well
that Basil is not indifferent to his opinion; but of the
three persons injured, it is Basil who is injured least.[34]

He can very well accept a reproof from a friend. He is
not so absurd as to be offended at the chidings of a
brother. Far from being offended, he well-nigh laughs
that when there were so many things which seemed to
strengthen and unite their friendship, his correspondent
should write that he has been so thunderstruck at small
matters,[35] and he is not in the least inclined to stand
upon his dignity, but will receive with the most perfect
submission any one who may be sent to investigate his

---

[32] Ep. ccxliv.
[33] Ep. ccxxiii.
[34] Ep. cciv.
[35] Ep. ccxliv.

supposed misdeeds.[36]

Like many other eminent men, Basil found a friend in his physician, and held the highest opinion of the profession. Humanity is the very business of those who practise the healing art, and that man who places their science first among all the pursuits of life, appears to Basil to judge rightly. But his doctor is not only perfectly accomplished in his healing art, but extends his benefits beyond the body and ministers to the mind.[37] Basil gratifies his affection for his friends by little presents, and they do the same by him. Wax candles and dry fruits seem to have been common gifts.[38] But Basil cannot use his teeth upon the latter: they are gone, through time and disease.

We can well understand what misery the distracted condition of the Church must have brought to a soul so full of piety and love. It was no spirit of proselytism that impelled Basil to work for Catholic unity, but a spirit of love. He can assert that there is in his heart such a longing for the peace of the churches, that he could willingly shed forth his own life to extinguish the flames of a hatred which the evil one has kindled.[39] So bitterly did the misconduct of many who should have known better weigh upon him, that he more than once confesses that a temptation to misanthropy had come over him, if the mercy of God, and the affection of a few stanch friends had not preserved him.[40]

Although it is laid down among Basil's monastic rules that it is beneath the dignity of a Christian man to

---

[36] Ep. cciii.
[37] Ep. clxxxix.
[38] Epp. ccxxxii., ccxci.
[39] Ep. cxxviii.
[40] Epp. ccxxiii., ccxliv.

laugh heartily, yet he himself was not at all devoid of a sense of humour. The theory of transmigration moves him to a gentle satire, perhaps not inapplicable to our own times, when he says that some philosophers declare themselves to have been once the men, women, or fishes of a far-back time; whether they were fishes or no he will not undertake to say, but that when they wrote these things they were more unreasoning than fishes he will very constantly affirm.[41] Nor could any writer devoid of this faculty have given us the description of the avaricious usurer swearing to the needy borrower that he has no money at all, and is himself looking out for some one to lend him a little; but when the other mentions the interest and the name of the security, then he smoothes his brow and smiles, and somehow comes to a remembrance of their family friendship, and says he will see if he can find some cash. "A friend, indeed, left a sum with me to be lent out in usury, but he requires very high interest." The debtor, on the other hand, has neither the wealth of the rich nor the careless freedom of the poor. He is constantly estimating the value of his own property, or of the plate and furniture of anybody with whom he happens to dine. "Were these mine," he says to himself, "I could sell them for so much and be free of my interest" If there is a knock at the door, he creeps under the bed. If any one runs up to him quickly, it gives him a palpitation of the heart. If a dog barks, he bursts into a perspiration. Why is interest called τόκος, that is, breeding? It must be called so from its immense fecundity of evil, or from the pangs which it brings on the poor people who endure it. Basil can even exercise a grim humour upon his own misfortunes, as when the

---

[41] Hexaem. Hom. viii.

vicar of Pontus threatened to tear out his liver, he replied, "Many thanks: where it is it has given a great deal of trouble." Nor is he above describing a disturber of the peace of the Church as the fat whale of Doara, who troubles the waters there. And it is thus that his friend Gregory describes his social character:—"Who made himself more amiable than he to the, well-conducted? or more severe when men were in sin? Whose very smile was many a time praise, whose silence a reproof, punishing the evil in a man's own conscience. If he was not full of talk, nor a jester, nor a holder forth, nor generally acceptable from being all things to all men and showing good nature, what then? Is not this to his praise, not to his blame, among sensible men? Yet, if we ask for this, who so pleasant as he in social intercourse, as I know who have had such experience of him? Who could tell a story with more wit? Who could jest so playfully? Who could give a hint more delicately, so as neither to be over strong in his rebuke nor remiss through his gentleness?"[42]

But his kindness to the poor and sorrowful is unfailing. The insensibility of the rich moves his bitter indignation. People lavish their money on unworthy objects; but if a poor man, scarce able to speak from hunger, comes into our sight, we turn from him as if he were of a different nature from us; we shudder at him, we pass by as if we feared that if we walked more slowly we might catch the infection of his misery. And if he looks upon the ground, filled with shame at his wretched state, we say that he is a hypocrite; and if he looks us boldly in the face, under the spur of his hunger, we call him an impudent and violent fellow. And if he

---

[42] We borrow Dr. Newman's translation. Church of the Fathers, p. 87 (Ed. 1840).

happens to be clad in whole garments, given him by
somebody or other, we send him away as insatiable, and
swear that his poverty is all a pretence; if he is covered
with rotten rags, we hunt him off as evil-smelling; and
though he ask us for God's sake, we will not be moved.
Yet Basil shows no weak pity. A helper who gives way
to the impulse of mere feeling seems to him like a pilot,
who, when he ought to be directing the crew and
fighting against winds and waves, is himself sea-sick.
We must use our reason, and help people as we can. Do
not therefore aggravate sorrow by your presence.
Whoever wants to raise up the afflicted, must be above
them: he who falls along with them, requires himself the
same aid which he is attempting to bring.[43]

Basil's recommendatory letters to his powerful
friends on behalf of the needy are often very moving and
graceful. Here is one on behalf of Leontius, who
apparently desires to escape some imposition of the
government. "There is no one closer to me, or who, if he
were in prosperity, would do more to aid me, than my
dear brother Leontius. Take care of his house just as you
would of myself, if you found me not in that condition
of poverty in which, by the Divine goodness, I am now,
but possessing some property. I know well that in that
case you would not make me poor, but would preserve
to me what I had, or increase it." Again, he begs that the
valuation of the property of a presbyter may not be
increased for higher taxation; "for he toils perseveringly
for the support of my life, because I, as you know, have
nothing of my own, but am supported by the resources
of my friends and relations."[44]

A similar description of Basil's mode of subsistence is

---

[43] Hom. quod mundanis adhær. non sit.
[44] Hom. in Mart. Julitt.

given in the succeeding letter, written on behalf of his
foster-brother, on whom he is dependent. But the
explanation is added, that Basil's parents have given to
this man most of the slaves whom he possesses, as a
fund for the support of their son.[45] These letters appear
to have been written before his episcopate; afterwards he
had resources at his command, though never for his own
benefit. He is much disappointed that a community of
monks, when burnt out, have not resorted to him as the
most natural refuge prepared for them.[46]

His own celibate life did not hinder him from
sympathy with family troubles. He has received a letter
from a bishop, which tells of the death of Urctarius's
only son. The heir of a great house, the prop of his race,
the hope of his country, the issue of pious parents,
brought up among a thousand prayers, in the very
flower of his age is snatched away from his father's
arms. But it is the bidding of God that they who have
faith in Christ should not sorrow for the dead; for they
believe in the resurrection. Some cause there is,
inscrutable to man, why some are carried soon away,
and some left longer to endure pain in this world of
troubles; we are not deprived of our son, but have
restored him to the Lender. Nor was life extinguished,
but changed; nor did the earth cover him, but heaven
received him. Only may we resemble his purity, that we
may learn that innocence which obtains the rest of
children in Christ.[47] And he knows how to comfort the
bereaved mother under the same loss. He was unwilling
to write, lest, even though he should give some comfort,
yet he might appear to intrude on her grief. But when he

---

[45] Ep. xxxv.
[46] Ep. cclvi.
[47] Ep. v.

reflected that he had to do with a Christian woman, long
since schooled in religion and prepared for troubles, he
thought it not right that he should be wanting in his
duty. A son she has lost, whom when he was alive all
mothers blessed, and wished their own to be like him;
and when he was dead lamented him as their own. We
are sad because he is taken away before his time. But
how do we know that it was not full time? We know not
how to choose what is most profitable for souls, and
define the bounds of human life. "Regard the whole
world in which we dwell, and consider that all things
that we see are destined to corruption. Beware of
measuring your calamity by itself: considered thus, it
will seem unendurable. Compare it with all human
things, so will you find comfort. And besides, I have
something to say which is the strongest thing of all.
Spare your husband. Be a comfort to one another. Do
not make his trouble harder by wearing yourself out
with grief. But, indeed, I do not imagine that words can
bring comfort; prayer is what is needed for such a time.
And I pray the Lord Himself to touch your heart with
His unspeakable power, to bring light into your soul by
holy thoughts, that you may have the spring of
consolation within."[48]

Basil in one of his discourses alleges, by way of
excuse for recurring to a subject left unfinished the day
before, a characteristic point in his own mental
disposition. He is by nature an enemy to anything
unfinished.[49] This extreme love of completeness is the
secret of his persevering labour, and of the manysided
activity which struck Gregory of Nazianzus, and which,
indeed, has rarely been exceeded. Among us, if a man

---

[48] Ep. vi.
[49] Hom. in Mart. Julitt.

be a student and a scholar, we do not at the same time
expect him to take a ruling share in the practical affairs
of the Church, and fight for her against the secular
power; if a man be a philanthropist and a founder of
hospitals, we do not wonder that he is not a great leader
of religious thought or a popular preacher. But Basil
displayed all these forms of activity in the highest
degree. Add to all his asceticism. Though we are,
perhaps, not very strict in applying the Apostle's
prohibition, "if any will not work, neither shall he eat,"
we at least use without stint the positive permission
implied by his words; and if any is willing to work for
us, we think it only his right that he should eat
abundantly of the very best. But Basil did all his work of
studying, preaching, travelling, visiting, hospital-
building and hospital nursing, and contending with
governors, emperors, and heretics, upon one meal of
vegetables and water in the day; and that, too, in spite of
constant ill health hanging about him from youth to age.
We feel compelled to believe that there never has been
an age of the world so rich in great intellects and great
hearts that Basil would not have justified his title to a
high place among them, nor are there many life-histories
to which we should more confidently point as examples
of the triumph of mind over matter, the spirit over the
flesh.

CHAPTER VI
A Picture of the Times

The idea which we derive from Basil's works of the
condition of the government in the Eastern Empire is by
no means favourable. The sentiment of patriotism, as
applied to the Empire at large, does not appear to have
existed in his mind. The misfortunes of the Imperial
arms under Julian, the threatening inroads of barbarians
under Valens, are alluded to much in the same way as
we should mention troubles of foreign powers; they are
warnings of the uncertainty of human things, and
lamentable events in themselves. Conquering armies, he
tells us, have been conquered in their turn, and become
spectacles of misery; great and victorious cities have
been reduced to slavery. The age just past has afforded
examples of every kind of calamity which the history of
the world records. But the writer shows no sense of
personal connection with them. He does love his
country; but it is Pontus, Cappadocia, or even Cæsarea,
to which he applies the term. It is well known that the
Greek race never extended its idea of political union
above the city; and certainly there was nothing in such
governments as those of Constantius and Valens to

enlist either the imagination or interest of the people in a wider conception of patriotism.

Basil had not, perhaps, personally very much to endure under Valens. But the failure to harm was, as the history of the affair proves, an example of the weakness and timidity of the Emperor and his officers rather than of their justice. And when his relations to them became amicable, the subjects of his letters to them give a very low notion of the equity and regularity of the administration. Now he writes to Aburgius on occasion of the division of the province, begging him by all his love for his native country of Cappadocia to assist her in her distress, which is such that no one who had visited her in former times would know her again.[50] Now he intercedes for an unfortunate old man who has been exempted by an imperial order from public service on account of age, but finds the boon immediately undone when the prefect claims his orphan grandson, aged four years, for some service or other to the council.[51] Now it is a request that oaths may not be demanded of the rural population in the exaction of the tribute, since it is a mere compulsion to perjury. Now the restoration is requested of some corn taken from a poor presbyter by some officer of the government, either on his own account or acting under orders. And now time is requested for getting in by a general subscription the gold which is to be paid as a tax for equipping the military. Or the widow Julitta is condoled with for the oppressions exercised on her by some official who has cast off all shame in his dealings with Christians, and she is informed that though Basil is afraid to take the liberty of writing directly to such a great man as the

---

[50] Ep. lxxx.
[51] Epp. lxxxiv., lxxxv., lxxxviii.

prefect, he has written to Helladius, a confidential member of his household, to make interest for her.[52] Or Modestus, the prefect, Basil's former opponent, is urgently pressed in the name of a poor down-trodden population to have the tribute of iron required from the miners of Mount Taurus reduced, that they may not be so utterly overwhelmed with poverty as to be rendered useless citizens to the State.[53]

It is not to be wondered at that under such a government the misery of the people should be very great. Basil writes, on occasion of the division of the province, that the order of society is quite broken up, that on account of the treatment dealt out to the magistrates the members of the civic administration have fled to the country, and their town, which formerly had been the resort of learned men as well as a place of wealth, had become a lamentable spectacle of decay.[54] It must, however, we may remark, have recovered under succeeding emperors, for Cæsarea, when sacked by Sapor the Persian, possessed 400,000 inhabitants. For the present the distress was widespread. Individuals met with reverses which reduced them from affluence to an abject condition; among whom Maximus, a man of great ability, and formerly prefect, having lost his whole paternal property and all that he had acquired by his own exertions, had become a beggar.[55] Basil is afraid, when writing to Eusebius in his exile, to entrust the messenger with anything of value, lest it should be the cause of his murder at the hands of some of the robbers

---

[52] Ep. lvii.
[53] Ep. cx.
[54] Ep. lxxvi.
[55] Epp. cxlviii., cxlix.

and deserters by whom the roads are infested.[56] We shall
hereafter read Basil's description of the horrors of the
famine which afflicted this unfortunate country; and he
also describes a grievous flood which has taken place in
consequence of a sudden thaw after a great fall of
snow.[57]

Amid these miseries of the poor, we find the greatest
excesses of luxury and selfishness among the rich. There
was, as usual in such states of society, the ill-omened
trade of keeping back corn till prices should rise to
famine point; and Basil warns the rich against being
"traffickers in human misery."[58] The legitimate methods
of trade were not developed. Basil mentions that he has
known of bankers in Alexandria who received money
and gave interest;[59] plainly implying that such a system
did not exist in Cappadocia. The methods of
investment, which in modern times are so close at hand,
being wanting, rich people were left,—if they did not
execute public works, or strive for popularity by shows
of wild beasts,[60]—to squander their money in luxury, or
to lay it out at usurious interest by lending it to their
needy or extravagant neighbours. And we shall see, in
several quotations from Basil's sermons, how prolific a
source of sin and misery was the recklessness of his
people in incurring debt. He compares the usurers with
their monthly demands of interest, to the demons who
inflict periodic attacks of epilepsy.[61] Meanwhile, others
spend their money upon numberless carriages or litters
borne by men, and covered with gold and silver.

---

56 Ep. cclxviii.

57 Ep. ccclxv.

58 Hom. in illud Luc. destruam horrea, 3.

59 Reg. brev. tract. interr. ccliv.

60 Hom. in Psal. lxi.

61 Hom. in Psal. xiv. 5.

Innumerable horses are kept, and their pedigrees are
esteemed according to the nobility of their ancestors,
just as those of men. Some are for riding about town,
some for hunting, some for journeys. Their reins, and
bits, and collars are of silver, adorned with gold. Purple
saddle-cloths deck the horses, like bridegrooms; there
are multitudes of mules paired according to their
colours, and their drivers in order one after another.
Troops of servants of all kinds—overseers, stewards,
gardeners; skilled workmen of every trade, whether of
necessity or luxury; cooks, confectioners, cupbearers,
huntsmen, statuaries, painters; artists of every species of
pleasure. Troops of camels, some for burdens, some for
pasture; troops of horses, herds of cows, flocks of sheep
and of swine, and their keepers; lands enough to feed all
these, and render a revenue to increase the riches of
their master. Baths in the city, and baths in the country.
Houses shining with marbles of all kinds; one encrusted
with Phrygian stone, another with Laconian or
Thessalian; and some of their houses arranged to keep
you warm in winter, others to keep you cool in summer.
Pavements floored with mosaic, ceilings covered with
gold; and whatever part of the walls is not inlaid with
marbles is adorned with pictures. And we may be sure
that the living was not inferior to the magnificence of the
houses. Sea and land were traversed in the search for
cooks and table-attendants,[62] who were brought like a
kind of tribute to the great people, and suffered miseries
in no way more endurable than the torments in Hades,
constantly stirring the furnace, bearing water, and
pouring it into a cask with holes; for there is no end to
their toil.[63] The ladies required jewels of all kinds—

---

[62] Hom. in Divites, 2.
[63] Serm. de legend, lib. Gent.

pearls, emeralds, jacinths, gold lace, and gold ornaments, and spent upon these things not a passing hour, but nights and days.[64] But sometimes Basil was able to gather from among these luxurious rich such converts as the two deaconesses, daughters of the Count Terentius.[65]

Among the multitude, the barbarous practice of exposing children to perish if the parents thought them too expensive to rear was by no means extinct;[66] and boys were frequently sold to slavery for their father's debts. The common talk of the people in the forum was of the most corrupting character. The religion of the common people was largely mixed with astrology and belief in charms. Basil reproaches even Christians as having recourse in the sickness of their children to some magician, who will hang a talisman round the patient's neck.[67]

No wonder that amidst such corruptions in general society the morality of the Church should have been far below the Gospel standard. The mass of the Christian population is represented to us as strangely alternating between self-denial and excess. The restraint of Church fasts is submitted to with a strictness scarcely known among ourselves; but it is succeeded by disgraceful outbreaks of drunkenness and impurity. Even in the midst of the fast Basil gives as a reason for protracting his sermon, that many of the congregation, when they are dismissed, will at once resort to the gaming-table, where they will experience all those alternations of fortune and all those exhibitions of passion which high

---

[64] In Div. 4.
[65] Ep. cv.
[66] Hexaem. viii. 6.
[67] Hom. in Psal. xlv.

play calls out. To what purpose, he asks, is it to fast if your soul be filled with such sinful impulses as these?[68] Nay, even in the churches themselves, miserable men but ill reflect the meaning of that glorious verse, which says that "in His temple doth every man speak of His honour." Instead of remembering and confessing their sins in God's house, they smilingly greet one another, and shake hands, and turn the house of prayer into a place of immoderate loquacity.[69]

The expulsion of Gregory Nyssen from his see by the eunuch Demosthenes, and the substitution for him of "a slave worth a few oboli," draws from Basil the vehement statement that the episcopate is fallen into the hands of born slaves.[70] Indeed, one extraordinary case is on record, in which a bishop was literally a slave. We have a portion (though unhappily not the conclusion) of Basil's correspondence with Simplicia, a great lady, who having been a large benefactress to the Church, became so proud as to maintain a claim to the ownership of a man, who, though belonging to a family of servile origin attached to her house, had been advanced to the episcopate.

Even among the clergy the greatest abuses prevail; and such a thing is known as a bishop going about without either clergy or people.[71] One case in the lower clergy gives us a notion of the class of people with whom Basil had sometimes to deal. A certain Glycerius had been ordained deacon by him. His qualifications were not high, yet he had considerable aptitude for routine work. But after ordination he wholly neglected

---

[68] Hexaem. Hom. viii. 8.
[69] Hom. in Ps. xxviii.
[70] Ep. ccxl.
[71] Ep. cclxv.

his duty, "just as if none whatever had been assigned to him." Worse still, he collected together a number of poor girls, some unwilling and some of their own accord; gave himself the airs of a patriarch, adopted this leadership as a way of making a livelihood, and caused the greatest disturbance in the Church, despising the commands of his presbyter, a man of age and character, of his chorepiscopus, and even of Basil himself. And when he was threatened with punishment for the bad example of disobedience which he was setting to several young men, he took to flight with his band. Certainly it was a most scandalous exhibition, when in the midst of a great crowd of persons this choir of young women was introduced dancing alternately with the youths, to the dismay of the pious and the amusement of the evil-disposed. And when the parents attempted to rescue these unhappy girls out of his hands, they were assailed with insult by this hopeful youth. Basil writes to Gregory, in whose diocese this worthy had fixed himself for the time being, begging that he may be induced to return, or at least send back such of the maidens as might wish to come back: if he declines, he is to be degraded from the ministry.[72] The next letter is to Glycerius himself; by no means too sharp a rebuke for the occasion, and encouraging him to return, with the promise of a kind reception if he repents. Another letter to Gregory follows: the girls have not yet returned, and we know not the conclusion of the affair.

Two epistles to Amphilochius, Bishop of Iconium, give us a conception of the steps by which church order was attempted to be restored in a district where everything had gone to confusion. It would be better if

---

[72] Ep. clxix.

bishops could be appointed to all the sees in the district;
but if good men cannot be found for all, the best plan
will be to send one bishop to preside over the whole
province, provided that he be a man of resolution and
courage, and one who, if he finds himself unable for all
the work, will engage others to his aid. If this cannot be
done, it will be wiser to commence with the small towns
and villages and work upwards from them, than to
appoint a bishop of the province who might possibly be
jealous of the restoration of the minor sees, when such a
measure should become possible.[73]

In his own diocese Basil found most serious abuses
prevalent. The chorepiscopi were wont to accept money
for ordination, cloaking their simony under the pretext
that they did not receive the fee until after the ordination
had been performed. Basil makes no parley with such
persons; they are roundly informed that they shall be
excommunicated in case of persistence.[74] We find our
saint lamenting the decay of primitive discipline in terms
which we ourselves might use, and with reason even
greater than we possess. According to the ancient
canons, no one should be ordained except after
examination into his character, had by the presbyters
and deacons of his neighbourhood, and reported
through the chorepiscopi to the bishop of the diocese.
But now the chorepiscopi were themselves accustomed
to ordain whomsoever the presbyters chose to send
forward, without examination of character, and often
simply for the purpose of escaping military service. So
that there were in many villages a multitude of clergy,
not one of them all fitted for his office: this is to be
absolutely altered for the future, and none to be

---

[73] Epp. cxc., cxci.
[74] Ep. liii.

ordained without submission of his name to Basil.[75] We have a severe letter to a presbyter reproving him for having a female dwelling in the house; it was not indeed a bad case, for the priest was seventy years of age, and Basil does not suspect anything wrong. We perceive plainly, in such cases, that the *mulier subintroducta* may have been often only a servant whom the priest employed for household convenience; but the rule against it was stringent and needful for the protection of the celibate life against suspicion, and she must be dismissed and placed in a convent on pain of anathema.[76]

When Basil takes a general view of the condition of the whole Church, it is gloomy indeed. Sometimes he compares it to a ship driven about by the fiercest storms, while the crew are quarrelling with one another;[77] and sometimes to an old robe, which it is very easy to tear wherever you touch it, but impossible to restore to its primitive strength and soundness[78] And yet we must by no means suppose that discipline was altogether extinct, or that church punishments were either unused or lightly regarded. On the contrary, Basil speaks of the ecclesiastical penalties as being equally effectual with those of the State. What the corporal punishments of the tribunals could not perform, he has known to be effected by the tremendous judgments of God.[79] And we find an example of this in a case of abduction, where Basil gives direction for the excommunication not only of the guilty man, but of the whole village which has harboured him.

---

[75] Ep. lv.

[76] Ep. lv.

[77] De Sp. Sanc., cap. xxx. 76.

[78] Ep. cxiii.

[79] Epp. lxxiii., cclxxxvi.

The penances which are prescribed in the canonical
letters of Basil are of much severity. For fornication four
years' penance is to be undergone: for one year the
offender is to be expelled from the prayers, and to weep
at the church door; in the second he is to be classed
among the "hearers"; in the third among the
"penitents"; and during the fourth he is to stand with the
people but abstain from the oblation; finally, he is to be
admitted to communion.[80] The extreme comparative
severity to women in the case of such sins which
modern society displays, is observed in these canons: the
man who has sinned is to be received back by his wife
on repentance; the wife by her husband, never. Basil
gives these directions from the ancient authorities, but
confesses that he cannot see the reason of them. A
widow who marries again is by the apostle's prescription
to be despised; but no law against remarriage is imposed
upon men. For them the "punishment of digamy"
suffices: that is to say, a penance of one year. While
second marriages are thus marked with a certain stigma,
third marriages are regarded as unlawful by the canons;
Basil speaks of them as existing but only as blots upon
the Church. A presbyter who unknowingly involves
himself in an unlawful marriage is to retain his seat
among the clergy, but not to be permitted to give the
benediction. This canon of itself implies that the
marriage of the clergy, though doubtless frowned upon,
and in the case of bishops becoming constantly less
usual, was neither prohibited nor unused. The allusions
in the epistles of St. Basil would lead us to suppose that
the present practice of the East—marriage for the parish
priests and celibacy for the bishops—represents pretty

---

nearly the state of things in his time. The question of marriage with a deceased wife's sister is carefully argued by Basil in an epistle to Diodorus, who had accused him of authorizing these unions. He decides against them on the sufficient ground that the voice of the Church is against them. The law of Moses does indeed say nothing applicable to marriage with the sister of a wife after the latter's death. But the principle that by marriage you acquire the same relations as your wife is decisive.[81]

In one point Basil increases the stringency of the ancient canons. The elder fathers had directed that a virgin who, after dedicating herself to God and professing a life of chastity, should marry, might be received after penance of a year. But in Basil's time, the monastic tendency having made a large advance, it seemed both possible and needful to go further; he directs that the marriage is to be counted as adultery, and the offender not to be admitted to communion until she has ceased to live with her husband. Professions of celibacy are not to be accepted from girls of tender years, nor from children brought by their parents or brothers, without any deliberate choice of their own. Sixteen or seventeen is the earliest age at which such self-dedication is to be accepted. No vows of celibacy by men are known, save of those who enrol themselves among monks, in whose case such an engagement is tacitly implied: and Basil is of opinion that it would be better to require of them a categorical profession clear and explicit, in order that if they marry they also may be punished as adulterers. This is an interesting canon, as showing the steps by which monastic vows became usual,[82] but the monastic system of Basil must be treated

---

81 Ep. clx.
82 Ep. cxcix. Canons 18, 23, 50, &c.

at large. Something of a passion for vows must have prevailed, since we find a prohibition of ridiculous ones, such as not to eat swine's flesh.

For murder we find prescribed in another epistle of this class the penance of twenty years' prohibition from communion; for adultery, that of fifteen; for apostasy, a man was to be repelled his whole life through, save that he might be communicated at death. But when we read of these very lengthened periods, we cannot but doubt whether they can have been in all cases really imposed and submitted to. And there are indications in the epistles of St. Basil that the system of discipline as it existed in his time must have admitted large modifications in practice. The Church by her canons marked her sense of the enormity of the sin; but in case of earnest repentance the Nicene council allowed the bishop to relax the rigour of the law. "If any one of those who have fallen into the prementioned crimes is very earnest and diligent in his repentance, he who is intrusted by God with the power of binding and loosing will not be to blame or without Scripture precedent if he regards the seriousness of the repentance as a reason for abridging the period of penance." And this was Basil's own practice. He "lays down these rules in order that the fruits of repentance may be well tested; but he is used to judge such matters not merely by time, but by the manner in which the penance is performed."[83] In truth, the state of the Church was daily making the ancient canons more and more difficult to maintain; and in writing to Peter, bishop of Alexandria, Basil considers it matter of thankfulness to find that in that place at all events some remains of the primitive discipline still

---

[83] Ep. ccxvii. Canons 74, 82.

existed.[84]

In circumstances so sad it cut Basil to the heart that
the Western bishops should show so little interest in the
case of their unhappy brethren. Not indeed but that the
list of churches with which Basil was in communion and
correspondence included the best part of the Christian
world.[85] Sanctissimus on one occasion even brought
from the West assurances of friendship; but this was all.
For thirteen long years the contest against heresy had
lasted, during which period Basil declares that more
evils had happened than were recorded to have taken
place since the foundation of the Christian Church. The
people had abandoned their houses of prayer and
assembled together in desert and solitary places; women
and little children were exposed to storms and snows,
winds and wintry ice, and heats of summer; and this
they had done that they might not be partakers in the
evil leaven of Arianism. The ministries of the Church
were in many places wholly in Arian hands. Baptisms,
the conducting forth of those going on journeys, the
visitation of the sick, the consolation of the sorrowing,
the teaching of the young; all these duties, which then as
now constituted the staple employment of the Christian
ministry, were exercised by the Arians, leaving little
hope that the succeeding generation of Christian people
brought up under such influences would be better than
the present. How comes it then that no letters of
consolation, no brotherly visit, none of those things
which the law of Christian kindness demanded, should
have come from the Western bishops? The miserable
condition of the East is known to all the world, and he
writes to the Italians as already aware of the miseries

---

[84] Ep. cclxvi.
[85] Ep. cciv.

which assailed their brethren. They should inform their emperor of the troubles, or if this were impossible, they should send some delegates who should visit and console the afflicted.[86] We have seen in the narrative of Basil's life that Valentinian did in fact interpose by promoting a council in Illyria, But it had no decisive effect in favour of the distracted East, in which peace was not restored until Basil, who had striven for it so earnestly and longed for it so passionately, was in his grave.

The decree of that Illyrian council, while implying the duty of the civil power to interfere for the maintenance of truth, yet lays down, as we have seen, with much stringency, the limits which the law of God imposes upon that interference. The same principles are expressed in the epistles of St. Basil. On the one hand we have a letter to the magistrates of an Armenian town, congratulating them that, amid their occupation with public cares, they do not forget or undervalue matters ecclesiastical, but are each as anxious about them as about their own concerns and the occupations on which their lives depend; and begs them to excuse the bishops for having been obliged in the difficulty of the times to take a course which might seem doubtful. But at the same time the principle is laid clearly down, that ecclesiastical administration is conducted by those who are intrusted with the government of the Church, and is confirmed by the people.[87]

Amid all defects we find that the worship of the Church was very hearty. If the sea be a beautiful thing, is not this crowded congregation more so, in which the mingled voice of men, women, and children follows our

---

[86] Epp. ccxlii., ccxliii.

[87] Epp. ccxxxviii., ccxxx.

prayer to God?[88] At the feast of a martyr strangers from
all sides were wont to assemble at his grave and wait
from over-night to midday beguiling the time with
hymns;[89] indeed, the antiphonal method of chanting
used under the influence of Basil, who seems to have
been very fond of music, was a subject of suspicion and
accusation to churches where different methods
prevailed.[90] The good old custom was still observed of
using at the lighting of the lamps the form, We praise
the Father, Son, and Holy Ghost.[91]

The constant tradition of the Church has been that
large reforms, not only musical but liturgical, were due
to Basil himself. M. de Broglie[92] is of opinion that the
general character of these reforms was a separation of
the offices in which all the faithful took part from those
especially reserved for priests. And he believes that the
extremely long form in which the Liturgy of St. Basil
has reached us is that which was intended for the clergy.
The character of that liturgy may perhaps be thus
roughly described for the English reader. He must
suppose a service far too long to be used in combination
with any other or with a sermon. He must suppose the
sacrificial idea which is expressed in the first of our post-
communion collects to be transferred to the ante-
communion, applied distinctly to the elements as
representing the sacrifice of Christ, and made the centre
for intercessions, supplications, memorials, and ritual of
a rich variety. He must suppose that an invocation of the
Holy Spirit, uttered at a point subsequent to the recital

---

[88] Hexaem., Hom. iv. 7.
[89] In Ps. cxiv.
[90] Ep. ccvii.
[91] De Sp. Sanc., cap. xxix.
[92] L'Eglise et l'Èmpire, v. 139 *sq.*

of the words of Institution, effects the consecration,
which with us is performed by those words alone. And
he must suppose the sacramental idea of participation to
come in at the conclusion, as the feast upon the
completed sacrifice, instead of being, as with us, the first
and leading idea of the service.

CHAPTER VII

Theology: The Doctrine of the Son

A very eminent writer has said that the controversies of the fourth century "were carried on, so to speak, in the scientific region, and did not greatly enter into the moulding of ordinary life and character."[93] No doubt this remark might be explained in some sense consistent with truth. But assuredly, if we were to apply it to the work of St. Basil in the region of theology, it would lead us quite astray. He was a great orthodox theologian, but he was a man of so pre-eminently practical a spirit, that if the theological controversies in which he mingled had not entered into the moulding of ordinary life, we may feel almost certain that he would not have touched them.

He grew up in the midst of the controversies upon the nature of the Son; and those upon the nature of the Holy Ghost had their origin during the period of his ministry. We have treatises from his pen upon both subjects; but there is the strongest proof of his moderation upon both, and of the fact that nothing but a clear and deliberate

---

[93] Mr. Gladstone in *Cont. Review*, Oct. 1878.

conviction of the vital importance of Catholic truth
could have induced him to lay aside the great works of
moral reformation and of charity which he had in hand,
in order to engage in the discussion.

Many of his oldest and best friends had been at some
period of their lives deceived by the plausible arguments
of Arianism, or semi-Arianism, or had been induced to
make concessions to error amidst the perplexities of
those difficult times. Gregory of Nazianzus the elder
had subscribed a semi-Arian creed, and so had Dianius
of Cæsarea, the beloved teacher of Basil's youth, whose
memory he regarded with love and reverence; Meletius
of Antioch had received Arian ordination, and Eusebius
of Samosata, than whom he had no closer confidant,
was tainted in a similar way. But the persecutions of the
reign of Constantius had afforded to many semi-Arians
an opportunity of suffering for their faith, which brought
them and the orthodox together; and Athanasius, as
well as Basil, was very ready to forget past errors in the
case of those who were now willing to draw to their side
for the defence of truth. We may be sure then that the
words of Basil which we have in this controversy are
those of one who had weighed well and charitably what
could be said upon the other side.

Upon the Arian controversy there was no question of
drawing up a new creed; that was sufficiently provided
by the creed of Nicæa, upon which Basil always takes
his stand, maintaining it on the one hand true, and on
the other sufficient. But the declarations regarding the
Holy Spirit which our creed contains were not yet
adopted by the Church. Basil repeatedly[94] recites the
Nicene creed, and declares that he will add nothing to it,

---

[94] Epp. cxxv., cxl., cclviii.

except a declaration that the Holy Ghost is not a creature, and that He is essentially holy, as are the Father and the Son. We find him[95] announcing his determination not to leave behind him any composition upon the faith; meaning thereby, we suppose, either a defined creed, or else a doctrinal treatise over and above those which he had already composed. This was a degree of moderation unusual at that period; for it was then that in some church, with which Basil must have been in close connection, the creed was cast nearly into the form to which we give the name of Nicene, and that other creeds were also propounded to supply the obvious insufficiency of the Nicene in respect to the controversies of the day.[96] Moreover, Basil drew upon himself the vehement suspicions and even open accusations of the religious world of his time by his apparent laxity on the doctrine of the Spirit; and we know from Gregory of Nazianzus that there existed at one time an understanding between the friends that Gregory should prosecute the controversy upon the Holy Ghost, while Basil should be silent, in order to give as few offences as possible to any committed to his charge. We may, therefore, be assured that what he was at last obliged to write upon this subject also was not the work of a controversialist, or of a thinker insensible to the evils of over-definition, but sober words forced from him by the practical needs of Christian truth.

The same idea of St. Basil's relations to Christian doctrine is impressed upon us by the position which the treatise *de Fide* holds to the *Moralia*. Were we sure that it was intended to be as it now stands, a preface to that work, it would inevitably bear the appearance, not

---

[95] Ep. clxxv.

[96] *See* the Second of Rev. F. A. J. Hort's Two Dissertations: Macmillan, 1876.

indeed of a moralist getting doctrine speedily out of his way, but of a Christian worker laying down briefly, decidedly, and beyond suspicion, the doctrinal principles of his work, in order to devote himself at leisure to that edifice of morality as a basis for which he values truth. Even if we suppose the *de Fide* to have been composed at an earlier period, this impression appears equally well based, and, on the whole, we can hardly be mistaken in viewing St. Basil as a man weary of strife and bent upon Christian living as the chief thing, yet driven to treat of doctrines because he believed that they did enter into the moulding of ordinary life and character, and was persuaded, as Professor Huxley expresses it, that "rational expectation and moral action are alike based upon beliefs."

The forms of error with which Basil had to deal were chiefly those of the Anomæans Aetius and Eunomius, who, without denying to the Son the name of God and divine worship, yet asserted His distinction in substance from the Father; of Sabellianism, which denied the reality of the distinction of persons in the Trinity, and regarded the various manifestations of the divine as only different appearances of the same one person, and the later heresy of the Pneumatomachi, which regarded the Holy Ghost as a creation of God, and in various other ways, often very difficult to grasp, denied the Catholic faith concerning the third person of the Godhead.

Basil's apprehension of the momentous practical danger of Arianism and Sabellianism is summed up in his repeated declaration that if we teach the existence of different beings of different substance, to whom we give the name of God and divine worship, we accept the principle of heathen polytheism, and if we teach the unreality of the personal distinction between the various

modes of manifestation of God, we are really returning
to Judaism. "Those who say that the Only-begotten is a
creature of God, and then worship Him and call Him
God, by adoring the creature and not the Creator, re-
introduce the errors of the heathen; and they who deny
that He is God of God, and nominally confessing the
Son of God, in reality and truth evacuate His existence,
renew Judaism;"[97] and a letter to the Western bishops,
describing the miserable condition of the East,
complains that there "Polytheism obtains; a greater and
lesser Deity are recognized. The Son is not a name
denoting His nature, but is considered as a title of some
kind of dignity; the Holy Ghost is not thought to
complete the Holy Trinity, nor partake the divine
nature, but to be one of the creatures, joined at random
and by chance with the Father and the Son."[98]

Basil's defence of Catholic doctrine is not based upon
any arrogant estimate of the knowledge we are capable
of attaining. Quite the reverse. "If I laid down that all
things were capable of being grasped by our knowledge,
I might be ashamed to confess my ignorance. But the
fact is, that not only are innumerable things of those
which are laid up for us in the future, or of those now
existing in the heavens, concealed from us, but we
cannot even understand clearly the things which exist in
our bodies. As, for instance, with respect to sight,
whether it is by receiving the images of visible things
that we form our perceptions of them."[99] Thus the
substance of everything is incomprehensible to us.
"What is the substance of the earth, and what is the

---

[97] Hom. xxiv. Contr. Sab. et Arian. et Anom.
[98] Epp. ccxliii.
[99] Adv. Eun., iii. 6.

method by which it is known?"[100] and if the substance of
all things is unknown to us, much more that of God.
"The peace of God passeth all understanding, yet
Eunomius will not allow that the very substance of God
is beyond all understanding and knowledge of man. For
my part, I believe that the conception of it passes not
only men's understanding, but that of all rational
creatures."[101] No one knoweth the Father save the Son,
and the Spirit searcheth all things; and what can this pre-
eminence in knowledge mean if any other can
comprehend the essence of the Deity. "It is under the
teaching of God's acts, and knowing the Creator
through His works, that we arrive at the conception of
His wisdom and His goodness."[102] And thus "there is no
one name which suffices to include the whole nature of
God."[103] "Names express not substances, but peculiar
qualities which characterize individuals. When we hear
the word Peter, we think not of his essence (I mean the
material substance), but of the individual qualities which
we perceive about him."[104]

What then is the meaning of declaring that the Son is
of one substance with the Father? "That one and the
same manner of existence is beheld in both; so that if,
for instance, the Father be thought of as being Light in
Himself and in His substance, we shall confess the
substance of the Son also to be Light."[105] Basil uses
repeatedly, in explaining this matter a form of
expression which at first sight is startling, namely, that
the distinction between substance (*ousia*) and person

---

[100] Ib. i. 12.

[101] Ib. i. 13, 14.

[102] Ib. l.c.

[103] Ib. i. 10.

[104] Adv. Eun., ii. 4.

[105] Ib. i. 19.

(*hypostasis*) corresponds to the distinction between common and proper nouns; as, "man" and "Peter."[106] So that the common nature which is designated by a common noun is common substance; and those proper nouns which are designated in general by the same common one are con-substantial.[107] Thus "all men are of one substance."[108] Plainly this is open to a misconception, which in fact was formed in the days of Basil; namely, that the assertion of the consubstantiality of the Father and the Son meant "a kind of division and distribution of a previously existing substance."[109] This objection was made by Paul of Samosata. But the answer lies in considering the nature of the substance of which we speak. "The idea might have some application to brass, and coins made of it; but, in the case of the Father and of the Son, the substance of one is not older than that of the other, neither can it be conceived as superimposed on both."[110] In fact, when you are dealing with perfect substance, the common appellation comes to denote a kind of unity, and an absence of separation, which it does not in the case of those substances which are limited and imperfect. We doubtless see in these passages of Basil the thoughts which were the germ of the contest between Nominalism and Realism.

Now the argument of Eunomius the Anomæan is based upon a refusal frankly to accept the knowledge which God gives us of Himself, going as far as He leads us, but confessing our ignorance where our knowledge really stops short. We grow weary as the argument of

---

106 Ep. xxxviii.

107 Ep. xxxviii.

108 Adv. Eun., ii. 4.

109 Ib. i. 19.

110 Ep. lii.

Eunomius is repeated in various forms, and pursued through infinite distinctions, that the epithet unbegotten expresses something which belongs to the substance of the Father, and that therefore the Son, who is admittedly begotten, cannot be of the same substance. But, replies Basil, "if the word unbegotten expresses the substance of the Father, so no doubt must also the terms immutable, invisible, and incorruptible. Now these confessedly are applicable to the Son: your argument therefore recoils upon yourself. For if these words express substance, then He to whose substance they apply must be consubstantial with the Father, to whom they also apply."[111]

St. Luke, in recording the generations, mounts from the later to the earlier, from Joseph to Heli, from Heli to Matthew, and so back to Seth, which was the son of Adam, which was the Son of God. In enumerating those, he surely does not indicate the essence or substance of the various persons named, but their origin. As he said then that Adam derived his origin from God, so we proceed to ask ourselves, "and God, from whom?" As every one must reply, "from none," we therefore call God unbegotten. Now if, in recording the human generations, their substance was not denoted, why should we suppose that God's substance is denoted by the denial that any generation took place in His case?[112] The word unbegotten expresses, not what the substance of God is, but what it is not.[113]

When we speak of generation in regard to God, we must think of a generation worthy of Him, and

---

[111] Adv. Eun., i. 8.
[112] Adv. Eun., i. 15.
[113] Ib. iv. 2.

impassible;[114] "that God out of His own divine nature, and in a manner becoming Himself, begat the Son, only-begotten, of equal honour and glory, sharer of His throne, His counsels, and His works; of one substance with God the Father, and not estranged from His sole Deity." Were the Son not all this, He ought not to be worshipped, for "thou shalt worship none other gods but Me."[115] He is the Word of God. But when we say Word we must not think of our methods of speech. God requires none such for His utterance. "The divine will and the first impulse of intelligent movement is the Word of God; out of the very thoughts of His heart, as one might say, comes the communication of His will."[116] And to introduce questions of time in relation to His existence is exactly as if one were to speak of what will happen after the death of an immortal being.[117] There are multitudes of expressions applied in Scripture to God, which we agree are to be tropically taken; as when we hear of God sleeping, being angry, flying, and the like; and shall generation be the only word into which we shall insist upon forcing a human meaning when we apply it to God.[118] We concede, it is true, that in one sense the Father must be placed before the Son; namely, in respect of the relation of a cause to that which it causes. But not in respect of difference of nature, nor yet in respect of priority of time. He said, "My Father is greater than I." But the Jews themselves interpreted the Lord better than Eunomius, when they accused Him of making Himself equal with God. And

---

[114] Ib. ii. 17.
[115] Ib. v. 5.
[116] Hexaem. iii. 2.
[117] Ib. ii. 17.
[118] Ib. ii. 24.

the Apostle declares, that He thought it not robbery to be equal with God. Plainly He uses the expression greater, because the Father is the cause of His being.[119] But it must be confessed that Basil elsewhere appears to reject this explanation of the verse, and to refer it to the voluntary honour which the Son pays to the Father.[120] And in still a third passage he argues that this very verse proves the Son consubstantial with the Father. For we make comparison of greater and less between things of the same nature, as between angels and angels, or men and men; and we cannot wonder that He who, by taking human flesh, made Himself lower than the angels, should say that His Father is greater than He.

He does, indeed, say, "As the Father said unto Me, even so I speak"; and "the word which ye hear is not mine, but His which sent Me"; and again, "As the Father gave Me commandment, even so I do." Not as if He were deprived of choice or will, or as if He waited for a preconcerted signal to commence His work; but He uses these expressions to manifest His own will to be inseparably adherent to the Father. Therefore when He speaks of commandment we must not understand an imperious injunction conveyed by physical organs, and giving directions regarding conduct to the Son as to a subject; rather must we think as becomes the Godhead, of a communication of will like the reflection of a form in a mirror, passing from the Father to the Son beyond the limits of time.[121] For "what time is to things physical that eternity is to the supramundane."[122] In truth, the declaration that He can do nothing of Himself is the one

---

119 Adv. Eun., i. 25.
120 Ib. iv. 3. [Some suspect the genuineness of the two last books.]
121 Ib. viii. 20.
122 Adv. Eun., ii. 13.

thing which proves Father and Son of the same nature. For all rational creatures can do something of themselves, for better or for worse: if the Son cannot, He is not a creature.[123]

"He was in the beginning with God." There are many beginnings of many things, but there is one beginning of all things, which lies beyond. Suffer your mind to range as far as it will, and stretch upwards; after numberless wanderings and vain endeavours, you will find it return back without any success in placing this beginning behind or beneath it. The beginning is ever found to be above and beyond our thought. In this beginning then was the Word.[124] And whoever thinks to lower the Son must needs apply the depreciating process to the Father also. For if he places the Father in the highest place, and supposes the Son to sit below, he is using a carnal method of imagination which must apply to the one divine person as well as to the other.[125]

The eye cannot use its vision beyond the region of light, nor can the mind use its faculty of apprehension beyond the Only-begotten. "Vain and blind and devoid of understanding is the mind which supposes itself able to apprehend the existence of anything before Him."[126] But in regard to the question raised by the term Anomæan; namely, whether the Son is like or unlike to the Father, it is to be observed that Basil does not profess to decide either way, but puts it aside as one which our faculties do not enable us to grasp. "We neither assert the Son to be like nor unlike to the Father; both of these are alike impossible. Like and unlike are

---

[123] Ep. viii.
[124] Hom. xvi. 1–2.
[125] De Sp. Sanc., vi. 15.
[126] Adv. Eun., ii. 16.

words which refer to qualities; now God is without qualities."

"Gird thee with thy sword upon thy thigh, O thou most mighty." Even so; for "that God should assume the nature of man is truly the greatest proof of His power. The formation of heaven and earth, of the ocean and the firmament, and the elements, and of things above the earth and things beneath, commends not the power of the Divine Word so much as His Incarnation and descent to the lowliness and weakness of humanity."[127] "He took upon Him the form of a servant." Had He been a creature, this could not have been said, for He would have been a servant already;[128] He took our flesh with all natural affections; but He did no sin. And as death, which was transmitted to us from Adam through our flesh, was swallowed up by the Deity, so was sin destroyed by the righteousness that is in Jesus Christ; that in the resurrection we might receive back again our flesh, neither subject to sin nor sentenced to death. These be the mysteries of the Church; these the traditions of the fathers. I testify to every man who fears the Lord, and looks for the judgment of God, that he be not carried about with divers doctrines. If any man teach otherwise, and consent not to the wholesome words of faith, but rejects the oracles of the Spirit, and considers his own teaching preferable to the doctrines of the gospel, such an one avoid.[129]

---

[127] Hom. in Psal. xliv. 5.
[128] Adv. Eun., iv. 1.
[129] Ep. cclxi.

CHAPTER VIII
Theology: The Doctrine of the Spirit

The heresy concerning the Holy Ghost which St. Basil had to oppose was, as he declares, unheard of in the Church up to his time. Montanus had propounded many false notions concerning Him, but had shrunk from calling Him a creature of the Son, as the Son a creature of the Father. It is impossible, Basil argues, that such a thing should be, were it but for this reason, that no operation of the Son can be separate from that of the Father, for, He says, "all mine are thine, and thine are mine."[130] We may remark, in passing, that it is difficult to see how, if the question of the Procession of the Spirit from the Son as from the Father had been before Basil, he could have resisted the twofold application of the principle which he here states, and of the text by which he supports it, as showing the impossibility of conceiving the Procession from the Father, if it was not also from the Son.

And the same may be said of another passage, which lays down that "as the Son is the Logos of God, so the

---

[130] Adv. Eun., ii. 33, 34.

Spirit is the word of the Son, who upholds all things, says Holy Scripture, by the word of His power. And since He is the word of the Son, therefore also that of God; as it is said, the "sword of the Spirit, which is the word of God."[131] And so again, he argues, that the Spirit could not bear witness with our spirits, that we are children of God, or cry Abba Father, unless He were really communicated by the Son, not sent by Him as a human spirit might be, but the everlasting Spirit of God and of the Son.[132] But it is to be confessed that the question of the twofold procession of the Spirit was not before the mind of our saint, and that nothing absolutely decisive on the subject is to be found in his writings. "The Son came forth from the Father, the Spirit proceedeth from the Father. But the Son is from the Father by generation, the Spirit, after an unspeakable fashion, from God."[133]

Basil's views of the operation of the Spirit in the universe of God are very noble. The Saviour is the Word of the Lord, the Holy Ghost the Spirit of His mouth, and both wrought together in the creation of the heavens, and the powers that are therein; wherefore it is said 'by the word of the Lord were the heavens made, and all the host of them by the breath of His mouth.' Nothing possesses holiness save by the presence of the Holy Ghost. The creative Word, the maker of all things, communicated being to the angels, and the Holy Ghost added holiness.[134] "There is no holiness without the Spirit. The heavenly powers themselves are not holy by their own nature; otherwise there would be no difference

---

131 Adv. Eun., v.
132 Ib.
133 Hom. contr. Sabell. 7.
134 Hom. in Ps. xxxii. 4.

between them and the Holy Spirit; but according to the proportion of their dignity they have their measure of sanctification from the Holy Ghost…. And they preserve their dignity through perseverance in good, possessing freedom of choice, but never falling out of the keeping of Him who is goodness essential. So that were you to withdraw the Spirit from their rational powers, the choirs of angels were broken up, the pre-eminence of the archangels destroyed, everything were confused, and their life reduced to disorder, lawlessness, and misrule. How should the angels say Glory to God in the highest, except through the power of the Spirit; for none can say that Jesus is the Lord but by the Holy Ghost, and none in the Spirit of God calleth Jesus accursed; which is what the evil spirits say, thereby confirming my principle that the unseen powers possess free will, equally capable of turning to virtue or to vice, and on this account requiring the aid of the Spirit. For my part, I believe that Gabriel himself could not foretell the future by any other means than the prescience of the Spirit, because prophecy is one of the gifts of the Holy Ghost."[135]

"He who would expel the Son [from the work of creation], expels the principle and source of the whole creation; for the Word of God is the source of existence to all things. And he who would expel the Spirit, would remove the perfection of things; since by the mission and communication of the Spirit all things are that are."[136] "You are to believe that in the creation of things, the primary Cause of all things is the Father, the efficient the Son, the perfecting the Holy Ghost…. Let no man suppose either that I am preaching three

---

[135] De Sp. Sanc., xvi. 38.
[136] Cont. Eun., v.

originating persons, or that I am declaring the working of the Son to fail in perfection. There is one Originating Principle of all things,—creating by the Son, perfecting by the Spirit."[137]

"The river of God, which is the Holy Ghost, makes glad the city of God, which is the church of those who have their citizenship in heaven; yea, all the rational creation, from the heavenly powers down to human souls, is in this city of God made glad by the river of the flood of this Holy Spirit."[138] "But as for the dispensation for the saving of mankind which, by the mercy of God, was performed by the great God and our Saviour Jesus Christ, who will deny that it was fulfilled by the grace of the Spirit? Regard either the blessings of the patriarchs of old, the help that was given to men through the Law, the types, the prophecies, the courageous deeds done in war, the miracles that were wrought by holy men, or the events which accompanied the advent of the Lord, they were done through the Spirit. For, first, He was present to the human body of our Lord Himself through His anointing, and was inseparably united to Him, according to the words, 'On whom thou shalt see the Spirit descending and abiding on Him, this is My beloved Son'; and again, 'Jesus of Nazareth, whom God anointed with the Holy Ghost.' Then every act of His was done by the presence of the Spirit, who was with Him when He was tempted of the devil, for Jesus was led up of the Spirit into the wilderness; was in closest union with Him in the performance of His miracles, for I, said He, by the Spirit of God, cast out devils; and left Him not when He rose from the dead. For when the Lord, renewing human nature, and rendering back to

---

[137] De Sp. Sanc., l.c.
[138] Hom. in Ps. xlv.

man again the grace which he had once possessed by the inspiration of the Spirit and had lost, breathed upon His disciples, what said He? 'Receive the Holy Ghost: whosesoever sins ye remit they are remitted unto them, and whosesover sins ye retain they are retained.' And the order of the Church is clearly, and beyond contradiction, carried on through the Spirit. For He gave, says St. Paul, first apostles, secondarily prophets, third teachers; after that working of miracles; then gifts of healing, helps, governments, diversities of tongues. For this order is arranged according to the distribution of the gifts of the Spirit."[139]

"Let us recount what our accepted ways of thinking concerning the Spirit are; as well those gathered from the Scriptures as those which we have received from the unwritten tradition of the fathers. Who then is not elevated in soul when he hears the very names of the Spirit. He is called the Spirit of God, and the Spirit of Truth which proceedeth from the Father—the right Spirit, the ruling Spirit. But Holy Spirit is His chief and distinctive title…. Impossible, therefore, that he who hears of the Spirit should frame the thought of a circumscribed nature subject to change or alteration or in any way like to a creature; but, mounting in thought to the very highest, he must conceive a rational substance, boundless in power, unlimited in greatness, immeasurable by times or by æons, unsparing in the dispensation of His good gifts. Unto whom all things turn when they need holiness; whom all things long after that live according to virtue, watered by His influence, and assisted unto the end which is their own and according to their nature. Perfecting everything,

---

[139] De Spir. Sanc., xvi. 39.

Himself in nothing deficient: Himself not living by
renewal, but the giver of life; growing not by accessions
but in His fulness at once stablished in Himself and
everywhere existent. The source of holiness; the
intellectual light; giving to every rational power an
enlightenment from Himself for the discovery of truth.
By nature unapproachable, yet comprehensible by His
own graciousness; filling all things by His power yet
communicable only to the worthy; communicated not to
all in the same measure, but distributing His energy
according to the proportion of faith. Uncompounded in
His essence, various in His powers; wholly present to
each and wholly present everywhere. Divided, yet
without suffering division; partaken by all, yet Himself
remaining whole, like a ray of the sun, which is present
to him who enjoys it as if to him alone, yet shines over
land and sea and is diffused into the air. Even so the
Holy Spirit, while He is wholly present with every one
capable of receiving Him, yet infuses into all a grace
complete and sufficient; so that all who partake of Him
enjoy Him as far as their own nature allows, but not to
the measure of His power.... He, like the sun, if He find
thine eye cleansed, will show thee in Himself the image
of Him who is invisible. In the blessed contemplation of
the image thou shalt see the ineffable beauty of the
archetype. From Him comes the uplifting of the heart,
the guidance of the weak, the perfecting of the
advancing. He shines upon those who are purged of
stain and makes them spiritual through communion
with Himself. And as light transparent bodies touched
by the sun become themselves aglow, and send forth
another splendour from themselves, so souls that bear
the Spirit, illumined by the Spirit, become themselves
spiritual, and transmit grace to others. Hence the

foreknowledge of things to come, the comprehension of mysteries, the discovery of secrets, the diffusion of gifts, the heavenly citizenship; the choral song with angels, the unending joy, the perseverance in God, the likeness to God; then, the summit of all desires, to become God."[140]

The proof of the deity of the Holy Ghost lies in this, that all of the operations and relations which are most peculiarly divine are ascribed to Him. If God be good, the Spirit is good by His very nature. If the Son be our Paraclete, He sends the Spirit to be such too. If Christ is our one master, the Spirit comes to teach us all things. If the Father and the Son distribute their gifts, so does the Spirit; as it is said there are diversities of gifts but the same Spirit; differences of administration but the same Lord; diversities of operations, but the same God, who worketh all in all: where we have to mark that the operation of the Holy Ghost is placed side by side with that of the Father and of the Son. And so again St. Paul says of God that He quickeneth all things; and Christ has the same power, for He says, "My sheep hear my voice, and I give unto them eternal life." Now, we are also quickened by the Spirit, as says St. Paul, "He that raised up Christ from the dead, shall also quicken your mortal bodies by His Spirit that dwelleth in you." Ye are built for an habitation of God by the Spirit. Can He then, by whom God dwells in us, be Himself of other nature than that of God? And our baptism is, according to the tradition of the Lord, into the name of the Father, Son, and Holy Ghost. He can be no creature and no servant who is thus united to the Father and the Son as completing the Godhead in Trinity.[141] And how can He

---

140 De Sp. Sanc., ix. 23.
141 Adv. Eun., iii. 5.

be called a servant who by baptism delivered you from servitude.[142] Must not the giver of renewal, who changes corruption into incorruption, who makes of us the new creature that abideth for ever, be God?[143]

Basil's treatise upon the Holy Spirit originated in the complaints (perhaps not at all unnatural) which some of his people made of varieties which he introduced into his doxologies in praying with them. Sometimes he was accustomed to ascribe glory to the Father with the Son and with the Holy Ghost; sometimes to the Father through the Son and in the Holy Ghost. Now it was from such a use of prepositions that the Pneumatomachi were accustomed to argue against the Deity of the Blessed Spirit. For they alleged that the preposition *by* indicated the maker of anything, as when we say that a bench is made by a carpenter; that *by means of*, or *through*, indicates the instrument, *e.g.* the axe which the carpenter uses; that *of* denotes the material of the work, viz. wood; and *according to*, the mental conception or the pattern to which the bench conforms; the word *for* expresses the final cause, as, for the use of man; and *in*, the time or the place of the making. Now Basil admits that he very often applies these prepositions; but he totally denies that they necessarily imply any such restriction of meaning. The Apostle applies to one divine person the very three prepositions which the heretics considered to be severally distinctive of the three persons: *of* Him, and *through* Him, and *to* Him, are all things. The Apostle writing to the Ephesians applies the preposition *of* to Christ, of (or from) whom the whole body groweth unto an holy temple. And it is also applied to the Spirit, as when the Lord says, that which

---

[142] Ep. viii.
[143] Adv. Eun., v.

is born of the spirit is spirit. *Through*, which they thought distinctive of the Son, is equally, in various places, used of each of the three persons. Christ was raised from the dead through the glory of the Father, and "that good thing which was committed unto thee keep through the Holy Ghost." And *in*, which they appropriated to the Spirit alone, and considered to mark His difference of nature from the Father and the Son, is used very often in reference to these; as (among many other instances) Paul and Silvanus and Timotheus to the church of the Thessalonians *in* God the Father.

The fact is, that we vary the preposition according to the relation in which the divine person to whom we apply it is at the moment felt to stand to us. For instance, when we contemplate the majesty and dignity of the Son, we give Him glory *with* the Father. When we think of the blessings which He has brought to us, we confess that this grace is wrought for us *in* Him and *through* Him. And so, indeed, it is with all the terms that we can apply to the divine persons—shepherd, king, physician, bridegroom, way, fountain, head,—all these describe not His nature, but the variety of His action.

Thus Basil's thorough knowledge of Scripture and his minuteness of detail, accompanied by large-minded good sense, furnish him with a very thorough answer to the ingenious arguments of his opponents. And his belief is summed up in these words:—Because those qualities which are common to all creatures are not shared by the Holy Ghost, and those qualities which belong to the Holy Ghost are not shared by the creatures, we infer that the Spirit is not a creature; because the attributes which are common to the Father and the Son are common also to the Spirit, because those points by which in Scripture the Father and the

Son are characterized serve also there to characterize the Holy Spirit, we infer that the Spirit is of the same deity with the Father. Because those properties which belong to the Father alone as God and not as Father, and to the Son as God and not as Son, belong also to the Spirit alone and not to the creature, so that names and acts unshared by the creature are common to the Trinity alone; we hence infer that the Trinity is consubstantial."[144] And this heavenly truth has this earthly action, that "our mind enlightened by the Spirit looks unto the Son and in Him as in an image beholds the Father."[145]

---

[144] Adv. Eun., v.
[145] Ep. ccxxvi.

CHAPTER IX
Theology: The Work of Salvation

Basil entertains by no means a low opinion of the natural condition of man. "The virtues," he believes, "are in us by nature, and there is an affinity of the soul to them untaught by men and due to nature itself. For as no instructions are needed to make us hate disease, and we have a natural aversion to things which give pain, even so the soul has an untaught aversion from vice, and all vice is a disease of the soul."[146] "And so it is not difficult for us, if we will, to conceive a love of virtue and a hatred of evil. For God has given every faculty to the natural soul for a good purpose; as that of love, so likewise that of hatred, in order that under the guidance of reason we may love virtue and hate vice. For there is a true and good use of hatred;—Do not I hate them, O Lord, that hate Thee?"[147] "And there is within the secret soul of us every one a balance, placed there by our Maker, whereby we can judge of the nature of things."[148]

---

[146] Hexaem., ix. 4.
[147] Hom. in Ps. xliv.
[148] Hom. in Ps. lxi.

And yet this balance is liable to error. "What if any man says 'my conscience does not condemn me'? This happens in bodily diseases. For there are many diseases of which the sufferers are not conscious; yet they trust the information of the physician more than their own insensibility. Even so also in the diseases of the soul, that is, its sins; even if one, not conscious of sins, does not condemn himself, he ought to believe those who see further into his state. The Apostles are an example of this when, in the fulness of their assurance that they loved their Lord well, they heard from Him, One of you shall betray Me."[149]

The awful question of the origin of evil presented itself to Basil as it has done to all thinkers. His general treatment of the question is optimistic; but at present we desire to note his particular account of the origin of man's sin. It is that which has occurred to so many others, that it comes from the abuse of liberty, which could not have been withdrawn from man without destroying his capacity for virtue. "Why is man capable of evil at all? On account of the free will which is suitable to his position as a rational being. Released from all constraint and receiving from his Maker a life which is free because he is made in the image of God, he perceives the good and knows the happiness of it, and has power, if he continues in the contemplation of the good and the enjoyment of spiritual blessings, to keep the life which is according to his nature; but has also power on occasion to turn from the good; ... therefore, expelled from Paradise, he was deprived of that happy life, and became evil, not of necessity but through folly.... As far as he departed from life, so near he

---

[149] Reg. brev. tract., Interr. ccci.

approached to death. For God is life, and to be deprived of life is death. So that Adam by his departure from God brought death upon himself…. Thus it was not that God made death, but we drew it on ourselves by our wickedness…. But why, it will be said, were we not at our creation made righteous? For the same reason that you yourself consider your servants dutiful to you, not when you hold them in bondage, but when you see them willingly fulfilling their duties to you."[150] "Adam by eating sinfully transmitted sin."[151] But still "he who against his will is attracted by sin ought to know that he is held in bondage by some sin previously committed by him, through his willing slavery to which he is carried forward by it even to sin which he does not desire to commit."[152] "Let us return therefore to the grace first given, from which we fell through sin."[153]

It is well known that the questions of original sin, of predestination, and the bondage of the will, never took hold of the mind of the Greek church as they did of the Latin. It need not be said that this was certainly not due to any superior subtlety in the West, or any deficiency on the part of the Easterns in readiness for difficult discussions. And so far as the Oriental element prevailed in the Church of the East, it may be shown by the case of Mohammedanism that high predestinarian doctrine would not have been naturally alien to its tendencies. But perhaps we may discern in the circumstance a phase of that deep-seated difference between the Greek and Latin mind which determined the progress of their political constitutions. Individualism was the character

------

150 Hom. Quod Deus non est auct. mal., 7.
151 Hom. in Famem, 7.
152 Moralia, Reg. xxiii.
153 Sermo Asceticus ad init.

of the one, organization of the other. To the Greek the idea of a great central government, binding vast multitudes into one and reaching to each individual, was not conceivable; to the Latin this was the very idea of the state. It may be that we discern the individualism of the Greek in religion as well as in politics. Basil in any case died long before the Pelagian controversy brought these questions distinctly before the Church. But we can feel a certain assurance that the passages above quoted involve principles which would hardly have inclined him to acceptance of the views of St. Augustine.

Basil's conception of Redemption will appear from the following:—"Seek not thy brother to redeem thee, but one who excels thy nature; no mere man, but the man Christ Jesus, who alone can offer a propitiation to God for us all, since God hath set Him forth to be a propitiation through faith in His blood. Moses was the brother of the Israelites, yet he could not make atonement for them.... He could not make atonement for himself. What can a man find of sufficient value that he should give it for the redemption of his soul? Yet was there found one thing, the equivalent for all mankind, which was given as a price for the redemption of our souls; namely, the holy and precious blood of Jesus Christ our Lord, which He shed for us all. Therefore are we bought with a price.... Though we were not His brethren, but were enemies through wicked works, yet He, being not man alone, but God, after He Himself has given us freedom, calls us brethren. He who redeemed us was, if we consider His nature, neither our brother nor man; but if we regard His gracious condescension to us, He calls us brethren and descends to humanity."[154]

In another place we find that view of the atonement which is more commonly regarded as the patristic; namely, that the sufferings of Christ were borne at the hands of Satan, who believed himself to be gaining full possession of the Son of God, and was deceived and defeated thereby. "The artifice which Satan planned against man turned out ill for himself, and what he had devised against humanity he proved to have unawares devised against himself: since he in no wise so much injured Him whom he hoped to estrange from God and from eternal life, as he did himself, made as he was an exile from God, and condemned to eternal death. And by the snare which he set for the Lord was he himself taken, crucified where he expected to crucify, and dying by the death whereby he hoped to destroy the Lord." But there is probably no real inconsistency between these views of the atonement. The sacrifice of Christ was offered to God: but the reason why such a death should have taken place is hid from us as part of the great secret of the pain and evil of the world, whereof Satan is the prince. It is plain therefore that while in one way the sacrifice of the Lord must be regarded as a free and pure offering to God, in another it must be thought of as an injury inflicted on Him by the evil which God mysteriously allows in the world.

He who believes in Christ is made by faith a son of God, worthy to be himself called a god, and is not judged. Sometimes, indeed, in Scripture the word to 'judge' means to *prove*, and sometimes to *condemn*. "Judge me, O Lord," the Psalmist says, meaning, as he himself proceeds to say, "prove and try me." "If we

---

[154] Hom. in Ps. xlviii.

would judge ourselves," the Apostle says, "we should
not be judged," meaning condemned.[155]

"Let nothing be to you an occasion of unbelief. If
thou considerest the stones, even they contain proof of
the power of their Maker; and so does the ant, the gnat,
the bee. In smallest things the wisdom of the Creator is
oftentimes displayed. He who stretched out the heavens,
and poured forth the mighty volume of the sea, He it is
who hollowed the minute sting of the bee to shed its
virus through. You must not say that anything was done
by chance.[156] But His judgments are like the great deep.
And if you ask why the life of the wicked is prolonged
and the days of the just shortened; why the wicked is
prosperous and the just afflicted; why the child is cut off
before its time; whence wars, shipwrecks, earthquakes,
droughts, and floods; why those things have been
created which are deadly to human life; why one is a
slave and another free, one rich and another poor, and
what requital is to be made by the Judge for all these,—
when these things come into your thought, remember
that the judgments of God are a great deep. But to him
that believeth is the promise given by God, 'I will give
thee hidden treasures of secret places.' "[157]

Such is Basil's mind concerning the blessings
imparted to the individual believer. And to every
believer an angel is assigned who is held worthy to
behold the face of the Father in heaven.[158]

Now let us see what he has to say concerning the
aggregate of the faithful—the Church. "God hath
blessed Thee for ever.... is manifestly spoken of the

---

155 Hom. in Ps. vii. 4.
156 Ib. xxxii. 3.
157 Hom. in Ps. xxxii. 5.
158 Ib. xlviii. 9.

Saviour as man. Or, since the Church is the body of Christ and He the Head of the Church; as I have said that the ministers of the divine Word are the lips of Christ, as Paul had Christ speaking in him so has every other who is Paul's equal in virtue; so all we, the rest, as many as have believed, are the members of Christ. So that were any one to refer to the Church the blessing given to the Lord, he would not be wrong. These words, therefore, 'God hath blessed thee,' mean He hath blessed thy members, and filled thy body with all His good things for ever."[159]

"On thy right hand did stand the queen in a vesture of gold, wrought about with divers colours." He speaks here of the Church, of which we read in the Canticles, that "she alone is the spotless dove of Christ, who conducts to the right hand of Christ those known for their good works, separating them from the evil, as the shepherd his sheep from the goats. The queen then stands by, the soul united to the bridegroom, even the Word, not dominated by sin, but partaker of the kingdom of Christ."[160] And "let not the Church of God, which has received the garment without seam, woven from the top throughout, preserved unrent even by the soldiers, and which has put on Christ—let her not rend her robe."[161] And "they who will not accept the ordinances of the churches elect of God, resist the command of God."[162] Thus Basil expresses that care for the unity of the Church, and that sense of the guilt of disobedience or of schism, which indeed his whole life exemplified. But his idea of ecclesiastical obedience, and

---

[159] Ib. xliv.

[160] Hom. in Ps. xliv.

[161] Hom. in Mamant. Mart., 4.

[162] Ep. ccxxvii.

of the greatness of the Church was far from being tyrannical or secular. He values it for the sake of the holiness of individual souls; and he gives to every holy soul a distinct part in church authority, and an assurance that all the promises to her will have their fulfilment individually to him.

The coming of Christ, whereby the present order of things will come to an end, will not be, as some suppose, a local or a carnal advent; we are bidden to expect an advent suddenly to take place throughout all the world in the glory of the Father.[163] And Basil's conception of the nature of the happiness of heaven and of the pains of hell is equally spiritual with his idea of the advent of the Lord. "It may be that the shame in which sinners are to live through eternity may be a more dreadful thing than the darkness and the eternal fire, where they will ever have before their eyes the traces of sin in their flesh, like some ineffaceable stain ever remaining in the memory of their souls."[164] "Brethren, do not imagine the kingdom of heaven to be anything else than the true contemplation of things which really exist; which the Holy Scriptures call happiness. For the kingdom of heaven is within you: and to the man within nothing belongs but contemplation. Contemplation, then, must be the kingdom of heaven. For we see now the reflections of things as in a mirror; but afterwards, when freed from this earthly body, and clothed with one which is incorruptible and immortal, we shall behold their archetypes."[165]

---

[163] Moralia, Reg. lxviii.
[164] Hom. in Ps. xxxiii.
[165] Ep. viii. 12.

CHAPTER X
Theology: Controversies of the Church

If we ask what side Basil would have taken in the Church controversies of the present day, we find that each of our parties might with much ease gather a catena of passages from his writings to favour its particular views. We have seen how strong his assertion is that the blood of Christ can alone atone for sin. He describes the true servant of God as putting no trust in his good deeds, nor expecting justification for his works, but placing his only hope in the compassion of God,[166] and again he declares that the true and genuine joy in God is when one is very humble about his own righteousness, and understands that he is altogether deficient in that respect, but is justified by faith in Christ alone;[167] and it would be equally easy to cite passages to show that he held Church doctrine upon the effect of the sacraments, upon the ministry of the Church, upon the nature of Church unity. But in truth, when we come

---

[166] Hom. in Ps. xxxii. 10.
[167] Hom. de Humil., 3.

from gathering texts to support certain doctrines to the much more important question, what proportion these doctrines held in his method of teaching and in his life, we find far more difficulty in classing him. If we might venture to express him in terms of our parties, we should say that he is much more addicted to preaching works than our Low Church, much less sacramental than our High, much more definite and ecclesiastical than our Broad; of course, each party is at liberty to contend that had he lived under the circumstances of the present day, he would have developed that part of his doctrine especially which it contends for. Though he has said the things above recorded concerning the nature of justification, we can by no means maintain that he uses the atonement as an instrument of conversion, or as a constant subject for Christian thought, in the way in which our great evangelical preachers have been accustomed to apply it. Though there is no doubt that he held sacramental doctrine, yet we do not find the sacraments used as motive arguments. The facts of regeneration and of the Real Presence are not brought to bear upon all Christians to reprove their sin, or encourage their hope, after the fashion to which many a great teacher has accustomed us now. The great subject of human duty is that which inspires Basil. To press this home, to pursue it in his own life into every minutest point, and draw others to follow him, this was what in that evil time he felt called to do. Not that he was a mere moralist; his zeal for holy works is inspired throughout with the most passionate love of Christ; it is never otherwise than intensely spiritual. But he is so intent upon the duty itself that he does not turn aside to connect it with doctrines, even where we might have expected that he must be led to do so. The doctrines for which he contended so earnestly were those which concern the nature of God; and, as we have above contended, he maintained these because he saw that they must have the greatest importance to human life; but what one might call the intermediate doctrines, which show how and by what process it is that human life connects itself with the truth about God, upon these he does not largely dwell. The particular necessities of his time had not called for the prominent development either of the doctrine of faith upon the one hand, or that of the sacraments upon the other, as making the connection between God and the Christian soul.

If, then, we proceed to state his belief and practice upon some of our controverted points, it is not that they occupied his mind in the same degree that they occupy ours. They are incidental matters with him; but the records of his own beliefs and those of his time upon them are not the less interesting to us.

Baptism he holds to have the remission of sins, and to bring to debtors the security of a free discharge:[168] he who is not baptized is not illuminated. For this reason he exhorts to speedy baptism. Every time is proper for obtaining salvation through baptism, and a most moving picture is drawn of the sad end of a man who has put off baptism until the last, and then, through the neglect of friends and the deception of a physician, who hides the approach of death, dies unbaptized.[169] But plainly Basil speaks of a state of things in which not only is adult baptism common, but a habit of deferring the rite prevails. Faith and baptism, he says, are two ways of obtaining salvation which are very closely linked

---

168 Hom. in Ps. lix. 4.
169 Hom. de Sanct. Bapt.

together.[170] We can see that the Church has not yet entered upon the practice of claiming all persons for God at the very opening of their lives, and giving them baptism as a testimony of His free love to them before ever they can consciously love Him. It is true that Basil's principles must in the end lead to infant baptism. For instance, where he argues that the Jew does not put off circumcision, but on account of God's command, and the threats to the uncircumcised soul, performs it on the eighth day, and asks, Shall we put off the circumcision not made with hands? it is plain that his argument and his analogy lead to the baptism of infants; and he lays down a principle applicable to all baptism, even that of hypocrites, when he says that although the Holy Spirit is not mingled with the unworthy, yet He seems in a certain way to be always present with those who are once baptized, waiting for their salvation through conversion, until He is finally cut off from the soul which profanes His grace.

It is not wonderful that the Church, suddenly put into a nominal possession of the Roman world, while conscious at the same time that her true adherents were only the few, should have hesitated to throw open her doors at once by the universal practice and preaching of infant baptism. A mass of her people only hung about her entrance, Christians in name, and yet not really such. It was natural she should delay to call them hers till there seemed some prospect of making the name a reality. But it is plain from what Basil says above on deferring baptism, as well as from many other testimonies from the history of the time, that deferring it by no means implied any depreciation of its value.

---

[170] De Sp. Sanct., xii.

Rather we should imagine ourselves to discern a superstitious overvalue of the formal rite, which led to much moral harm.

With regard to the rebaptism of heretics, Basil evidently feels a strong sympathy with the views of Cyprian which enjoined that practice. The Cathari, Encratitæ, Hydroparastatæ, separated from the Church, had, he believes, no longer among them the grace of the Holy Spirit, the communication failing as the apostolic succession had been cut off. Those who first separated had ordination from their fathers, and by imposition of their hands possessed the spiritual gift. But they who were cut off, having become laity, had neither power to baptize nor ordain, nor could communicate to others the grace of the Holy Spirit, from which they themselves had fallen. Wherefore Cyprian and Firmilian and their adherents directed that the members of these sects, when returning to the Church, should be purified by the genuine baptism of the Church. But since it has seemed to some in Asia that for the sake of wise management of the multitude the baptism of these heretics should be accepted, be it accepted.[171] But in another place we find that this principle is forbidden to be extended to those sects which were infected with Marcionite theories of the essential evil of matter. For if they make God thus the author of something essentially evil, their use of His name in baptism must be a mere mockery. "Therefore," says Basil, "if rebaptism is generally forbidden among you, as it is among the Romans for the sake of some policy, let however our dictum bear its weight with resect at least to these."[172]

We shall devote a special chapter to Basil's

---

[171] Ep. clxxxviii.
[172] Ep. cxcix.

conspicuous faith in Holy Scripture and his loving use of it. But this did not in him imply any disbelief in the existence or value of church tradition. He commences his work against Eunomius by saying that if all Christians could have been content with the tradition of the Apostles he would have had no need to write. And again, "Let the tradition warn us all not to separate the Holy Ghost from the Father and from the Son. For so the Lord taught; the Apostles preached; the fathers preserved the deposit, and the martyrs sealed it with their testimony."[173] It is with Basil an important thing that his belief should agree with that of the great majority. But this great majority includes not merely the Christians that now are, but those who have been since the time that the Gospel was first preached. And this tradition is to be gathered from the ways of speech which have been handed down not in one particular church, but everywhere "both in town and country."[174] "Of the dogmas which are preserved in the Church, there are some which we have from Scripture, others we have received from the tradition of the Apostles, and both have the same force; nor will anybody contradict them who has any experience of the laws of the Church." But the sequel shows that the traditions thus spoken of refer to practices or to such teaching as is embodied in practices, rather than to formal doctrines. "For if we go about to reject the unwritten customs as of slight importance, we shall unawares do injury to the vital parts of the Gospel itself, or rather, reduce the preaching of it to a mere name. For instance (to mention in the first place what comes first of all and is most common) who has taught us by writing to sign with the

---

[173] Hom. contr. Sabell., 6.
[174] De Sp. Sanct., vii.

cross those who place their hope in Christ? What Scripture has taught us to turn to the east in the prayers? The words of invocation, when the bread of the Eucharist and cup of blessing are consecrated, which of the saints has left to us in writing? For we are not content with those words which the Apostle and the Evangelist record, but, both before and after, we use others and consider them to possess great importance to the mystery; and these we have received by unwritten teaching. And we bless both the water of baptism and the oil of unction, and even the very person who is baptized. Out of what Scripture? Is it not on account of the silent mystical tradition? The very anointing with oil itself, what written record has taught? And whence received we the custom that the man should be thrice immersed? And the rest of the ceremonies in baptism, as the renouncing of the devil and his angels, whence have we....? For this cause we all look to the east in our prayers; but few of us know that in doing so we seek our native land Paradise, which the Lord planted in Eden, toward the sun-rising. And we pray standing on the first day of the week, not only because, being risen together with Christ, we should seek those things which are above; but because that day appears to be a type of the world for which we hope."[175]

Concerning confession we find one passage which would seem to indicate that Basil regarded it as an outward and public act of self-mortification, to be resorted to only in the case of very flagrant sin. "Hast thou reviled: then bless. Hast thou extorted: then restore. Hast thou been drunken: fast. Hast thou been proud: humble thyself. Hast thou been envious: exhort.

---

[175] De Spir. Sanc., cap. xxvii. 66.

Hast thou killed: suffer martyrdom, or, what is equivalent to martyrdom, afflict thy body by confession."[176] Yet it would be very hasty to assume this to be a sufficient account of the matter, for again we find confession spoken of as the universal means of return to God: "If thou desire by confession to return to God, avoid drunkenness, lest it alienate thee more from Him." We find him applying the term confession to the solemn public acknowledgments of general sin which he and his fellow-worshippers made in the time of famine. In his monastic rules Basil directs that even every thought of the mind should be divulged to those brethren who are appointed for the gentle and sympathizing treatment of the diseased souls.[177] And indiscriminate confession to all is forbidden.[178] It is to be made to those to whom is intrusted the dispensing of the mysteries of God. For so in old times they who repented are found to have done before the saints; it is written in the Gospel that they confessed their sins to John the Baptist; in the Acts, to the Apostles themselves, by whom also they were all baptized.[179]

But while we find these directions concerning confession in Basil, it must be observed that the general tenor of his teaching is by no means what some would call sacerdotal. Of course he held those beliefs concerning the priesthood which were accepted in his time, and which we find incorporated in the Liturgy which bears his name. But the offices of preaching and teaching, with the accompanying duty of holy example, form the side of the Christian ministry which occupies

---

[176] Hom. in Ps. xxxii. 2.
[177] Reg. fus. tract., Interr. xxvi.
[178] Reg. brev. tract., Int. ccxxix.
[179] Reg. brev. tract., cclxxxviii.

his chief attention. When we read among the Moralia that "they who are intrusted with the preaching of the Gospel ought with supplication and prayer to appoint, whether deacons or presbyters, without reproach and of approved life," we seem to ourselves to be reading an ordinance of some Reformation church, and taking the view of the offices of bishops and clergy which we should expect to find in it.[180] And "he who is elected" is not, on the one hand, to preach until he be licensed, nor, on the other, to put off obedience when he is called to preach.[181] Those hearers who are instructed in the Scriptures ought to put to the proof what is said by their teachers; to receive what is agreeable to the Scriptures, and to reject what disagrees. What Basil's views were concerning the priesthood of the clergy and that of the laity we see from his answer to the question "whether the saying, 'if thou bring thy gift to the altar,' applies to priests alone; and how every one of us offers a gift at the altar." It is, that "it is reasonable to refer the words [only] in a special and primary sense to priests, since it is written, *ye shall be called priests of the Lord, the ministers of our God;* and, *the sacrifice of praise honoureth me;* and again, *the sacrifice of God is a troubled spirit;* and again the Apostle says *that ye present your bodies a living sacrifice, holy, acceptable to God, which is your reasonable service;* every one of which things is common to all. And whatever is of this kind everybody is bound to perform."[182] But the passage above quoted in respect to baptism, concerning the failure of the gifts of the spirit in schismatical bodies after the first generation, shows how strongly Basil held the doctrine of Apostolical Succession.

---

[180] Moralia, Reg. lxx.

[181] Ib.

[182] Reg. brev. tract., Interr. cclxv.

Upon the Holy Eucharist we find him alleging the Lord's words in St. John 6. to prove that participation in the body and blood of Christ is necessary even to eternal life itself. But he proceeds to point out that he who comes to communion without a perception of the manner in which the body and blood of Christ are given receives no profit; and he who eats and drinks unworthily is condemned. The manner in which we are to eat the flesh and drink the blood of the Lord is explained to be, in remembrance of His obedience unto death, that they which live should not henceforth live unto themselves, but unto Him which died for them and rose again.[183] It would be difficult to prove that Basil had formulated any theory of the manner of the Presence in the Eucharist.[184] Concerning the practice of reception we have a letter from Basil in answer to a lady who has consulted him about the expediency of daily communion. He pronounces it to be thoroughly good and useful. For when the Lord Himself says, "He that eateth My flesh and drinketh My blood hath eternal life," who can doubt that to be continual partaker of life is to live in a manifold way? His own custom he declares to be to communicate four times a week; namely, on Sundays, Wednesdays, Fridays, and Saturdays, and on any other days also on which the feast of a saint may fall. He proceeds to solve a scruple about taking the communion with one's own hands in time of persecution, when no priest or deacon is present. This he declares plainly right; and customary also, as in the case of hermits. For when once the priest has perfected the sacrifice and distributed it, he who receives it and takes daily a portion of what he received, may well

---

[183] Moralia, cap. xxi.
[184] Ep. xciii.

consider that he is daily receiving it from the priest's hands.

In his preface to the "Moralia," upon the judgment of God, he dwells upon the evils of schism in a way which would certainly have led him to point to an infallible earthly guide had he known such a one to exist. In his wide experience of life he declares himself to have observed that in every art and science the best understanding is maintained among those who are devoted to its pursuit. In the Church of God alone, for which Christ died, and upon which the Holy Spirit has been abundantly shed, he has observed a great and exceeding dissension in the mass, both as to their relations to one another and to the Holy Scriptures; and what was most terrible, the rulers of the Churches themselves took part in the dissensions. When he sought the cause of this lamentable condition, he remembered the case of the Jews when there was no king in Israel, but every man did that which was right in his own eyes. And this, strange though it appears, he believes to be most truly the case among Christians, and that all this schism arises because men have revolted from the one great and true and only King and God, our Lord Jesus Christ. The good order and agreement of the people he has observed to continue so long as the rulers of the Churches themselves obey in common the one chief. Why was the Church united in one body? That discipline and order might the rather be maintained in her of whom it was said, "Ye are the body of Christ, and members in particular": for that the one and only Head, who is Christ, governs and unites each to each. And, again, we find him recording how the Lord constituted Peter, after Himself, shepherd of the Church, saying to him, "Feed my sheep"; and adding, that He extends equal authority to all pastors and teachers after.[185] If we cannot maintain these passages to have been aimed at the pretensions of the bishop of Rome, the only reason is that we cannot suppose those pretensions to have been at the time so put forward as to require them. But they, when combined with the record which we have in his letters of his actual relation to the Pope of his day, sufficiently show on which side Basil would have been if the controversy on the supremacy and on the infallibility of the Pope had arisen in his time. If these doctrines be true, we are driven to the conclusion that this great saint was absolutely ignorant of a part of the Christian religion which if true must always be the most important part of all, but in Basil's time would have assumed even more than usual prominence on account of the confusion and separation which reigned supreme through the whole East.

In truth, there is almost nothing in the genuine writings of St. Basil which in the least degree jars with the beliefs or devotional habits of a faithful Anglican churchman. He cannot have believed in purgatory who exhorts us to believe that the separation of soul and body is liberation from all evil, and so bids us await the enjoyment of everlasting bless, ings, whereof all the saints have been made partakers.[186] He cannot have been a believer in the immaculate conception[187] who asks, what need had there been of the Holy Virgin if it had not been necessary that the god-bearing flesh should have been taken out of the lump of Adam.[188] Basil applies the Lord's prophecy, "All ye shall be offended because of

---

[185] Const. Monast., cap. xxii.

[186] Ep. xlii. 4.

[187] Epistle ccclx. to Julian is beyond question spurious.

[188] Ep. cclxi. 2.

Me this night," to a fluctuation of mind which His death should bring not only to Peter but to the Blessed Virgin herself.[189] Nor is there anywhere in his works to be found one slightest hint of the intercession or intervention of the Blessed Virgin in any shape whatever.

There is one marked exception to the general agreement of Anglican theology to that of Basil in the value attached by him to relics of the martyrs, and in the point therewith connected of resort to the intercession of martyrs at the place of their sepulture. He promises Arcadius, a bishop who was engaged in building a new church, to find him, if it be possible, some relics of martyrs, and expresses great interest in the matter.[190] To a relation in Scythia he suggests, that as persecution is said in that country to be even still providing martyrs, his correspondent should send some relics of them to his native land.[191] To St. Ambrose he writes, sending at the request of that saint the body of Dionysius, bishop of Milan, and affirming with great emphasis the genuineness of the remains.[192] In preaching upon the feast of the Forty Martyrs of Sebaste, he exhorts his hearers to have recourse to their intercession, and records miracles to have been effected by its means.[193] But it is to be remarked, that this belief in our power to call the intercession of martyrs to our aid is strictly connected by Basil with the place where their remains lie. He bids all those who *in this place* have found the martyr Mamas a helper in their prayer, to remember

---

[189] Ep. cclx.

[190] Ep. xlix.

[191] Ep. civ.

[192] Ep. cxcvii.

[193] Hom. in Quadrag. Mart. The chief church at Tirnova, lately recovered for Christian worship from the Mahommedans, is dedicated to these forty martyrs.

him.[194] He declares that the body of the martyr Jullitta, buried in the beautiful church of the town, confers sanctity both on the place and on those who pray there.[195] And thus his idea upon the subject involves merely a very emphatic recognition of that feeling which is so natural to us all, that we are brought nearer to the dead when we visit their graves, combined with a belief that the saints in glory are certainly engaged in intercession. And an argument which he uses for the deity of the Holy Ghost seems to prove that he had never thought of extending his belief in the intercession of martyrs or saints to all places indiscriminately, or endowing them with that practical omnipresence which a general practice of invoking them involves. Other heavenly powers, he says, are confined in their operations each to one place. The angel who stood by Cornelius did not at the same time stand by Philip; nor did the one who spoke to Zacharias at the altar fill at the same time his place in heavan. Whereas the Spirit is at one and the same time present with Habbakuk and Jeremiah in Palestine, with Daniel in Babylon, and with Ezekiel by the Chebar; and does not this presence in various places at the same time prove His deity?[196] It seems impossible that any man accustomed to invoke saints whom he knew at the same time to be invoked by Christians in other places, should have advanced this argument without some anticipation of the obvious retort.

---

[194] Hom. xxiii. 1.

[195] Hom. in Mart. Julitt., 2.

[196] De Spir. Sanct., cap. xxiii.

CHAPTER XI
Theology: Questions of the Day

We have to face deeper problems in our day than those which concern controversies in the Church; and in conversing with the works of a great thinker of the past, the thing we most desire to find is the information which he may have to give us upon these vital questions. Let us select from the writings of St. Basil two or three specimens of his thoughts upon the difficulties which oppress us. To us the cardinal problem of all is that of Theism or Agnosticism. And some readers of Hamilton, Mansel, and Herbert Spencer, may possibly imagine this doubt to be an invention of these later times. But the reader will judge whether it did not in its essential nature come before Basil, and whether he shrank from facing it.

"Do you worship something which you know, or something which you do not know? If we answer, We worship something which we know, the rejoinder is immediate, What, then, is the essentia of the object of your worship? But if we confess that we do not know this essentia, they retort upon us, So then you worship something which you know not. But we reply, that this

112

word "know" has different significations. For we say
that we know the greatness of God, and His power, and
His wisdom, and His goodness, and the providence with
which He guards us, and the justice of His judgments;
but not His very essence. He who confesses that he
knows not the essence of God does not thereby confess
ignorance of a God the conception of whom is brought
near to us by all these things which I have enumerated.
But God, they say, is uncompounded; and whatever in
Him you regard as known, belongs to His essence. This
is a sophism. For of all these attributes which we have
mentioned, shall we say that they are all names for the
one essence, and that His awfulness and His kindness,
His justice and His creative power, His prevision and
His retribution, His magnificence and His providence,
are equivalent to one another; and that whichever of
them we speak of, we speak of His essence? For if they
say that, let them not ask us if we know the essence of
God, but whether we know that God is awful, just, or
merciful: for we say that we do know that. But if they
say that essence is anything else, let them not mock us
by talking of His uncompounded nature, when they
themselves assert essence to be different from these
attributes."

"Which comes first, knowledge or faith? We reply,
that in education faith generally precedes knowledge;
but in our doctrine, if anybody says that knowledge
precedes faith, we shall not differ with him. For in
education you must first believe that this letter is an
alpha, and when you have learnt the characters and
pronunciation, then you come to the accurate
knowledge of the power of the letter. But in the faith
which is conversant about God, the thought that God is,
leads the way, and this we know from the creation. So

we receive Him as our Master; for since God is the Maker of all the world, and we are a part of the world, He is our Maker. And faith follows this knowledge, and worship this faith....

"We profess that we know so much of God as can be known, and that we know also that something escapes our apprehension. As if you were to ask me if I knew what sand is, and I were to say, yes, you would manifestly charge me falsely with ignorance, if immediately you require me to tell you the number of grains of sand. The sophism is the same as if one were to say, Do you know Timothy? Well, if you know Timothy, you know his nature: give us an account of it. I know Timothy, and do not know him according to the signification of the word 'know' which you adopt....

"If it be otherwise, how does St. Paul say, 'Now I know in part?' This is impossible if God is regarded as uncompounded. Do we know His whole essence? How then does he add, 'when that which is perfect is come, then that which is in part shall be done away'? 'The ox knoweth his owner,' says the prophet; and so, according to you, the ox must know the essence of his master."[197] From these extracts we perceive that Basil was aware of the difficulties and apparent contradictions to which men's imperfection condemns them in their knowledge of religion, but also that he recognized that basis of necessary knowledge of God which lays in each human soul a natural foundation for religion. And the same appears from the following extract, in which truthful and careful thinking are not less apparent than passionate devotion.

"The love of God cannot be taught. We did not

---

[197] Epp. ccxxxiv., ccxxxv.

learn from any one else to take pleasure in the light nor to desire life. No one taught us to love our parents, or our nurses. Thus, or rather far more, the learning of the love of God comes not from without, but along with the constitution of life (I mean the life of man) a certain seminal power of reason is in-grafted in us, which possesses from its own store the means of that appropriation which leads to love. Which power the school of the divine commandments takes in hand, tills with care, nourishes with skill, and by the grace of God brings to perfection.… Whatever commandment God gives us, we have received beforehand from Him the power of performing.… And the definition of vice is the evil use, against the divine command, of what He has given us for a good end.… Since, therefore, we have received the commandment to love God, we possess the loving power sown in us at our primary constitution, and the demonstration comes not from without, but every one may learn it from himself and in himself. For we naturally love the beautiful, though to different persons different things may seem beautiful; and we have an untaught love of that which is related to us and is brought close to us, and we delight to display all good to those who do us good. Now what more admirable than the Divine Beauty? What conception more attractive than the magnificence of God? What longing so vehement and irresistible as that which is engendered of God in the soul which is purged of vice, and which cries out of unfeigned desire, I am sick of love?.… This beauty cannot be discerned by the eyes of flesh, but is apprehended by the soul and mind alone; and when it shines upon a saint, it leaves in him an irresistible longing; for in their weariness of the present life, some have said, 'When shall I come and appear before God?'

and 'to depart and be with Christ is far better'; and, 'My
soul is athirst for God, yea, even for the living God';
and, "Now, Lord, lettest Thou Thy servant depart in
peace'…. For through their insatiable longing after the
Divine Beauty, they made supplication that their sight of
the pleasures of the Lord should extend itself throughout
eternity.

"Whatever, therefore, can be accomplished by the
operation of our will is also in us by nature, if we have
not perverted our thoughts by sin. And so the love of
God is required of us as a debt due of necessity, and the
absence of love is to the soul that wants it the most
intolerable evil. For alienation and aversion from God is
worse than any torments of hell, as the privation of light
is to the eye, even if no pain be present, or the
deprivation of life to a living thing. And if children
naturally love their parents, let us not seem more
unreasoning than children, being without love for our
Maker, whom even if we could not know from His
goodness to be what He is, yet we ought to love for this
reason alone, that we are made by Him. But among
those who are naturally loved, the greatest benefactors
hold the first place…. Now the goodness of the Master
never deserted us, nor did we hinder His love by
undervaluing all His gifts; we were recalled from death,
we were quickened to life again by our Lord Jesus Christ
Himself…. He took our infirmities and bore our
sicknesses, He was wounded for our transgressions, and
by His stripes we are healed: He redeemed us from the
curse, being made a curse for us: He endured a most
shameful death that He might restore us to the glorious
life…. And He is so good as to exact no recompense, but
is satisfied if He be merely loved for what He gave. And
when I think of all these things (to reveal my heart's

desire), I fall into a kind of terror and ecstasy of fear, lest ever, through inattention of mind or occupation with vanities, I should fall from the love of God and become a reproach to Christ.… The reproach which our fall will bring on Christ and the glorying of the enemy seems to me worse than the punishments of hell; that we should afford to the foe of Christ matter of boasting, and occasion of pride against Him who died for us and rose again."[198]

Surely no man ever possessed a loftier or more generous religion than this.

It may interest the reader to know how Basil thought upon the great question of Future Punishment. The query is proposed,[199] "If one shall be beaten with few stripes, and another with many, how say some that there is no end of punishment?" The answer is as follows: "Those things which, in certain places of inspired Scripture, appear doubtful and obscurely expressed, are cleared up by other passages which are admittedly plain. When the Lord, therefore, in one place declares that these shall go into everlasting punishment, and in a second sends some away into everlasting fire prepared for the devil and his angels; and in another place names hell fire, and adds, where their worm dieth not and the fire is not quenched,—since these and such like passages are found in many parts of inspired Scripture, it is one of the devices of Satan that the mass of mankind, as if forgetful of these declarations of our Lord, should prescribe an end to punishment, in order to encourage themselves in sin. For if there shall once be an end of punishment, eternal life also shall clearly have an end. And if we cannot endure to think this of life, on what

---

[198] Reg. fus. tract., Interr. ii.
[199] Ib., cclxvii.

principles shall we assert that eternal punishment will end.... This being confessed, we perceive that the words, he shall be beaten with few stripes, and he shall be beaten with many, do not indicate duration but difference in the nature of punishment. For if God be a just judge, rendering to each not only of the good but also of the wicked, according to his works, one may be worthy of inextinguishable fire, yet this may be of a gentler or fiercer power of burning; and one of the worm that dieth not, yet this again causing a milder or a sharper pain according to his deserts; and one may be worthy of hell, yet hell may easily have different punishments; and another of outer darkness, where some may be in weeping alone, and others also in gnashing of teeth, on account of the severity of the pains. And that outer darkness plainly indicates that there is an inner darkness too. And the expression in Proverbs, the depth of Hades, shows that some are in Hades, but not in the depth of Hades, enduring a lighter punishment One may illustrate this by the case of bodily diseases as we know them now. For one man shall have a fever with aggravated symptoms and other sufferings; a second suffer from simple fever, and this not in the same way as another man; another has no fever, but some pain in his limbs, and this again in a greater or less degree than another."

Whatever value may be attached to St. Basil's treatment of the subject, the manner in which he approached it is plain. He was not insensible to its awful difficulties, but the method by which his mind sought relief from them was not that of anticipating degrees in the duration of punishment, but by conceiving all kinds of possible degrees of punishment, to some of which the epithets soft and mild might be applicable. On one point, at all events, his authority cannot be disregarded. Upon the meaning of the words æon and æonial it is equal to that of an English scholar of the present day upon the meaning of the English of the time of the Reformation.

As closely allied to this subject we may give St. Basil's conception of the nature of evil and of the nature of punishment. "If evil is neither uncaused nor caused by God, whence has it its being? For that evil exists no one who has life will deny. What do we say then? That evil is not an existence living or animated, but a disposition[200] of the soul contrary to virtue, produced in the inert on account of their fall from the good."[201] "Evil is the privation of good."[202]

"This must also be said, that we do not punish those who have done wrong on account of what has been done; for what device can there be by which what is done can be undone? We punish them that they may be made better for the future, or that they may be an example to others."[203]

---

[200] διάθεσις,—an Aristotelian word; see Metaph., 4, 19.
[201] Hexaem., Hom. ii.
[202] Hom. Quod Deus non est auctor malorum.
[203] Ep. cxii.

CHAPTER XII
The Christian Life

It is our purpose to gather together in this chapter some aphorisms upon the Christian life from the works of St. Basil, which may serve to give the reader some idea of the practical use which he made of the principles of his theology.

It is his opinion that the religious life commences almost necessarily in fear. "The fear of the Lord is the beginning of wisdom, and they who have given themselves to earthly tastes must be instructed by fear. Fear is of necessity applied as leading the way to piety, and love afterwards taking in hand those whom fear, the instructor in knowledge,[204] has brought to order, perfects them."[205] And yet fear is very far from being the ideal condition of the Christian soul. "If ever a ray of light falling upon thy heart hath inspired thee with a sudden thought of God, and illumined thy soul with a love of God, with a contempt for the world and all bodily things, then from that dim and passing image

---

[204] Ἐπιστημόνικος, an Aristotelian word.
[205] Hom. in Ps. xxxii. 6.

understand the abiding condition of the just, their equable and unfailing joy in God. To you in the providence of God this joy comes at long intervals, that by this little taste He may bring thee into remembrance of what thou art deprived. But to the just this divine and heavenly joy is constant, because the Spirit dwells in them once for all, and the first fruit of the Spirit is love, joy, and peace."[206]

And this is St. Basil's notion of what is meant by glorifying God. "He who with unconfused and piercing eye can discern the truth himself, and after having himself discerned it, can make known to others all which concerns the goodness of God and His just judgment, he it is who gives glory and honour to the Lord, and who lives a life in harmony with such a contemplation."[207]

With wonderful freshness he sets before us the example of Christ. "In well-nigh every action which leads to blessedness the Lord led the way, and proposed Himself as an example to His disciples. Consider the Beatitudes, and as you examine them each you will find that He anticipated by His acts the instruction which His words convey. Blessed are the meek. And how shall we learn meekness? 'Learn of Me,' he says, 'for I am meek and lowly of heart.' Blessed are the peace-makers. And who has taught us the beauty of peace? He, the peace-maker, who has reconciled both into one new man, and has made peace by the blood of His cross, both among things in heaven and things on earth. Blessed are the poor; and it is He who became poor and emptied Himself, and took the form of a servant, that we might

---

[206] Hom. in Ps. xxxii. 1.
[207] Ib. xxviii. 2.

all receive of His fulness, and grace for grace."[208]

The true dignity of man is learned in Christ. "If thou rememberest not thy first origin, conceive the estimation of thy worth from the price that was paid for thee; look at thy ransom, and thence know thy value. Thou wast purchased with the precious blood of Christ; be not the servant of sin."[209]

But, alas! the spirit in which Christian people do their work falls far below the height of their calling. "We, if we imagine we have kept even one only of the commandments (yet I would by no means allow that we can keep but one, since they all hang together so closely according to the true scope of the Bible, that when one of the least is broken the others are of necessity broken also), instead of expecting blame for all that we have broken, expect reward for the one that we have kept."[210]

St. Basil was accustomed in his day to behold terrible downfalls in lives that had been full of promise. "Many who had laid up much spiritual wealth from their youth, and have arrived at middle age, when temptations arise against them by the machinations of the evil one, have not succeeded in resisting the weight of the tempest, but have lost all. Some concerning faith have made shipwreck; others have cast away the chastity treasured from youth under some sudden hurricane of sinful pleasure which has rushed upon them. A most piteous spectacle: that after fasting, after self-denial, after long prayer, after plentiful tears, after the continence of twenty or thirty years, a man should, through an unwatchful spirit and carelessness, be made a show of,

---

[208] Ib. xxxiii. 5.
[209] In Ps. 48:8.
[210] Reg. fusius tract., Prooem.

naked, and stripped of all."[211]

Human discontent abounded in those times as much as in the days of Horace or in our own. "People take no account of those who are worse off than they, nor feel gratitude to the Giver of good for the blessings they have; but, computing their wants by comparison with those above them, they are as querulous and complaining as if they were deprived of something that properly belonged to them. The slave is discontented because he is not free; the free man because he is not of high family and cannot count up seven generations of ancestors, illustrious breeders of horses, or who spent their wealth upon gladiators. The man of good birth is aggrieved because he has not plenty of money; the rich man chafes because he cannot obtain posts of authority over cities and peoples; the general because he is not a prince; and the prince because he has not the command of all things under the sun, but still some nations remain which are not subject to his sway. And so it comes to pass that none of them return thanks to their benefactor for any of their blessings."[212]

"How may one escape the vice of man-pleasing, and disregard the praise of men? By full assurance of the presence of God; by the persevering study to please God; and the fervent desire of the blessings to be found in God."[213]

"May one ever use an economy of truth, and lie for some good purpose? The sentence of the Lord allows no such thing; for He said that a lie is of the devil, and made no difference between one lie and another. And the Apostle said, 'If a man strive for the mastery, yet is

---

[211] Hom. in Princip. Proverb., 16.
[212] Hom. in Mart. Julitt.
[213] Reg. brev. tract., Interr. xxxiv.

he not crowned, except he strive lawfully.' "[214]

"How must we deal with those who avoid indeed the greater sins, but make no account of committing the smaller? In the first place we must know that in the New Testament no such distinction is to be found. For there one sentence lies against all sins in the declaration of the Lord that he that committeth sin is the servant of sin.... On the whole, if we may speak of great and little sins at all, it is beyond controversy that the sin by which each man is overcome is great to each, and that which he is master of, small; just as among athletes he that overcomes is the stronger, and he that is overcome is weaker than his conqueror, whoever he be."[215]

"When the Lord says 'Give alms of such things as ye have, and behold all things are clean unto you,' does He mean that all sins which a man may have committed are cleansed through alms? He means all sins which we commit through avarice and rapine. Zacchæus gave half his goods to the poor and restored fourfold anything that he had taken. So that whatever sins are of this kind, that it is possible to do away with their effects and restore fourfold for them, may so far be cleansed in this way. I say so far, since this in itself is not sufficient for cleansing, but itself needs in the first place the mercy of God and the blood of Christ, in whom also we have redemption from all others if we bring forth worthy fruits of penitence for each."[216]

The following conveys St. Basil's conception of a Christian's prayer:—"There are two kinds of prayer: one, that of praise and humiliation; the other, and the lower, that of petition. When thou prayest, then, come

---

[214] Reg. brev. tract., Interr. lxxvi.

[215] Ib. ccxciii.

[216] Reg. brev. tract., Interr. cclxxi.

not at once to petitions. If so, thou bringest on thyself
the suspicion of having resorted to God under the
pressure of necessity. When thou beginnest to pray,
leave aside thyself, thy wife, thy children; let go the
earth and pass the heavens; leave behind every creature,
seen or unseen, and begin by glorifying Him who made
all things. And when thou glorifiest Him, be not
distracted in mind here and there, nor recount fables like
the heathen, but draw from the Holy Scriptures and say,
'I bless Thee, Lord, the patient, the long-suffering,
which every day bearest with me a sinner, and givest us
all the opportunity of repentance. For therefore thou art
silent, O Lord, and bearest with us, that we may glorify
Thee who providest for the salvation of our race, and
hast visited us now by terrors and now by warnings,
now by prophets, and lastly by the coming of thy Christ.
For Thou hast made us and not we ourselves. Thou art
our God.'

"When thou hast blessed the Lord out of Scripture
according to thy power, and hast sent up thy praise to
Him, then begin to humble thyself and say, 'I am not
worthy, O Lord, to speak before Thee, because I am a
sinner.' Even though thou knowest nothing evil of
thyself, thou must speak so; for none is without sin, but
God only. For many though our sins are, the largest part
of them we do not ourselves understand; therefore saith
the Apostle, 'I know nothing by myself, yet am I not
hereby justified.' Wherefore thou dost not lie if thou
callest thyself a sinner; for if, knowing thyself to be a
sinner, thou sayest that thou art not one, thou sinnest in
this very saying. Say rather, I am a sinner, above all in
that I transgress the divine command, 'When thou hast
done all things that are commanded thee, say I am an
unprofitable servant.' … And when thou hast completed

the two parts of prayer, praise and humiliation, then for
the rest ask what thou needest to ask, not riches, nor
earthly glory, nor health of body. For He made thee and
careth for thy salvation, and knoweth how far it is
expedient for each either to be in good health or to be
sick; but ask the kingdom of God and things worthy of
it. And when thou askest things worthy of God, give not
over until thou dost obtain them."[217]

St. Basil believes that we may in real truth pray
without ceasing. "Not in syllables, but rather in the
intention of the soul and in acts of virtue, which extend
to all the life, is the power of prayer.… When thou
sittest down to table, pray; when thou takest food, give
thanks to Him that gave it thee; when thou supportest
thy weakness with wine, remember Him that gave thee
that gift to make glad thy heart. When the time of taking
food has passed, let not the memory of the merciful
Giver pass too. When thou puttest on thy coat, thank
Him that gave it thee; and when thy cloak, increase thy
love to God, who provided us with garments fit for both
winter and summer. Is the day over? Thank Him who
gave us the sun for the service of our daily work, and
gave another fire to lighten the night and serve the rest
of the needs of life. Let night afford other suggestions of
prayer. When thou lookest up to heaven, and seest the
beauty of the stars, pray to the Lord of all things seen,
and adore the all-merciful Artist of the whole, who in
wisdom hath made them all. And when thou seest all
living things buried in sleep, then again worship Him
who even against our will breaks off by sleep the stress
of our toil, and, by a short respite, restores our
strength.… Thus mayest thou pray without ceasing, not

---

[217] Const. Monast., i. 3.

in words, but by the whole conduct of thy life, so uniting thyself to God that thy existence is an unceasing prayer."[218]

And thus he treats the corresponding duty of thankfulness. "In everything give thanks. But how does it come that a command is given us the performance of which does not depend upon our own will, but is the result of external causes? Shall I give thanks when put to the torture; when I have received an insult; am frozen with cold; deprived of my children, or even of my wife herself?… But the Apostle exhorts to continual thanks not everybody, but the man such as he himself was, no longer alive in the flesh, but who has Christ living in him. This close contact with the supreme good things does not admit the feeling of the unruly affections of the flesh.… The soul which is once endowed with the longing after the Creator, and is accustomed to the delights which are to be found in it, would by no means exchange its joy and delight for the motley variety of carnal passions, but from those things which are sad to others will derive an increase of joy. Such a one was the Apostle, who took pleasure in infirmities, in reproaches, in necessities, in distresses for Christ's sake … and think how many just occasions of joy the mercy of God affords to us. We were brought into being out of nothingness. We were made after the image of the Creator. We have mind and reason to complete our nature, whereby we can know God. And as skilled observers of the beauty of the world we recognize by it, as by a document, the providence and wisdom of God. We can discern good from evil. We are taught by Nature itself to select the useful and to avoid the

---

[218] Hom. in Mart. Julittam.

harmful. Estranged from God by sin, we were called
again into His family and rescued from our shameful
slavery by the blood of the Only-begotten. The hope of
resurrection, the enjoyment of angelic blessings, the
kingdom in the heavens, the promised good things
surpassing both thought and speech, are ours.[219]

How may we hinder wandering thoughts in prayer?
"By being fully certain that God is before your eyes. For
if when you see a prince or ruler, and converse with
him, you keep your eyes fixed on him, how much more
shall he who prays to God keep his mind fixed on Him
who searcheth the heart and reins, according to the
Scriptural precept to lift up holy hands without wrath
and doubting."[220] Yet wandering thoughts, if
involuntary, must not induce us to give up prayer. "If
thou standest before God as thou oughtest to do, and
performest thy duty as thou canst, cease not until thou
receive thy request; but if thy conscience condemns thee
of negligence, and if thou standest for prayer with
wandering spirit when thou mightest be collected, dare
not so to stand before God, lest thy prayer be sin. But if,
weakened by sinful habit, thou canst not pray without
distraction, put a force on thyself all thou canst, and
persevere in standing before God, keeping thy mind
directed towards Him, and recalling it to itself, and God
will pardon thee that, not through contempt, but
through weakness, thou canst not appear before Him as
thou oughtest."[221] "And even though in the midst of thy
prayers the evil one should suggest wicked imaginations,
let not thy soul give over praying, nor think that the evil
seed sown by the tempter, and the various imaginations

---

[219] Hom. de Grat. Actione, 2.
[220] Reg. brev. tract., cci.
[221] Const. Monast., i. 4.

of that subtle magician, are the produce of the soul itself; but reflecting that these thoughts are suggested by the impudence of the inventor of evil, be the more instant in prayer, and ask of God that the fabric of evil thought, built up by the memory, be broken down, so that without hindrance, by a sudden impulse of the mind, thou mayest pass to God."[222]

We cannot love God truly without loving man. "Who knows not that man is a gentle and a social creature, not solitary [monastic] or rude. For nothing is so proper to our nature as to associate with one another, and to need each other's aid, and to love our kind. And where God has sown the seed, He demands the fruit.… Wherefore, through the first command we may execute the second; and again, by means of the second return upon the first; and when we love God, love our neighbour as a consequence.… So that Moses desired to be blotted out of the book of God, if pardon were not extended to the people for their sin, and Paul dared to pray that he himself might be accursed from Christ for his brethren's sake: filled with the desire to be like his Lord, a ransom for the sins of all: yet knowing, at the same time, that it was impossible that one who had rejected the gracious gifts of God through love to Him, and for the sake of keeping the greatest of the commandments, should be estranged from Him—nay, should not for that reason receive manifold more from Him. But to such measure of love to men could the saints arrive."[223]

Fasting (including therein abstinence from wine during the time of the fast) is, according to Basil, an absolutely essential part of Christian life. "It is not

---

[222] Const. Monast., xvii. 2.
[223] Reg. fus. tract., Int. iii.

possible, without fasting, to dare approach the sacred rites; not merely in the true and mystical service of the Church, but even in that typical worship which was offered under the law."[224] Take care, however, that you do not suppose fasting to consist in abstinence from food alone. For the true fast is estrangement from evil. Loose the bands of iniquity. Forgive to thy neighbour the wrongs done to thee: forgive him his debt to thee. Fast not for strife and debate. Thou eatest no flesh, but thou devourest thy brother. Thou abstainest from wine, but dost not refrain from insults. Thou takest no food until the evening, but spendest the day before the tribunals. Woe to them that are drunken, but not with wine."[225]

With what fear, and what assurance, and what dispositions of mind should we receive the Body and Blood of Christ? "The Apostle teaches us fear, saying, 'He that eateth and drinketh unworthily, eateth and drinketh condemnation to himself': and assurance is secured by our faith in the words of our Lord Himself; 'Take, eat, this is my body which is given for you; do this in remembrance of Me'; and in the testimony of John, who first tells of the glory of the Word, and then introduces the method of the Incarnation in these words, 'And the Word was made flesh and dwelt among us, and we beheld His glory, the glory as of the only-begotten of the Father, full of grace and truth.' "[226]

Basil longed for death. "Hearest thou not David say, bring my soul out of prison. Hearest thou not of a holy man, that his soul was set free (Tobit 3:6, 15). And what said Simeon, who took the Lord into his arms? 'Lord, now lettest Thou Thy servant depart in peace.' For to

---

224 Hom. de Jej., 6.
225 Ib., 12.
226 Reg. brev. tract., Interr. clxxii.

one who hastens to the life above, continuance in the
body is more oppressive than any punishment or any
prison."

CHAPTER XIII
The Lover of Nature

We should be omitting one of the most characteristic points in the works of Basil if we were to pass without notice his love of nature. It is to him instinct with religion. God said, "Let there be light," "and this word was a work, whence sprang nature, than which human thought can imagine nothing more delightful to enjoy."[227] "Believe that the voice of God is effective of nature, and that the command then given to the creature prescribed to created things the sequence of the future."[228] "If ever in the calm of night, gazing at the unspeakable beauty of the stars, thou didst take thought of the Artist of the whole, who He is who adorned the heavens with these flowers; again, if in the waking thoughts of the day thou hast learnt the wonders of the day, and through things seen conceived things unseen, thou comest a fit hearer to occupy this awful and blessed theatre."[229]

---

[227] Hexaem., Hom. ii.

[228] Ib. Hom. iv.

[229] Ib. Hom. vi.

The precept "Let the earth bring forth," is still immanent in nature, and prompts her every year to put forth the powers which she possesses to produce herbs, and seeds, and trees; for as whirlwinds from the first impact make their succeeding gyrations, when fixing a centre they revolve within themselves around it, so the sequence of nature, deriving its commencement from this first command, goes forward to all succeeding time until it comes to the common end of all things. To which let us also hasten, bringing forth our fruit, and full of good works, that, being planted in the house of the Lord, we may flourish in the courts of our God in Jesus Christ our Lord.[230]

That man was not insensible to the spirit of nature who could thus describe the ocean, which from the summit of Mount Argæus, above Cæsarea, can be discerned in the Black Sea and the Mediterranean to north and south. "A pleasant sight is the whitening sea when a steady calm possesses it: pleasant, too, when gentle breezes roughen its surface, and impart to it a purple colour or a blue, as we behold it, when it smites not its neighbour land with violence, but salutes it as it were with a gentle embrace."[231] He is aware that "the Western sea has its tides, now retiring, now returning, as if drawn upwards by the respirations of the moon, and pressed back as she breathes out again."[232]

He has a very just sense of the relations of man to nature. On the one hand, he warns us against imagining that everything was made for us, or that we are to judge of the uses of things merely by the effect which they have upon our pleasure or profit "What, then! shall we

---

[230] Hexaem., Hom. v.
[231] Ib. Hom. vi.
[232] Ib.

omit to offer our thanks for what is beneficial to us, and yet impeach the Creator on account of those things which are injurious to our lives? Shall we not confess this, that all things were not made for the sake of our appetites?"[233] But, on the other hand, he has an ennobling conception of man's position in the world. "By nature earthly, but the work of God's hands, in strength falling far short of the brutes, but the appointed ruler of all senseless and soulless things; inferior in natural equipment, but able by the excelling gift of reason to rise to heaven itself."

Basil was both an observer of nature himself and careful to gather information from all who could give it After describing the habits of those fish which at certain seasons ascend the streams and return, "which things," says he, "let us hear from the mute ones," he proceeds to tell us, "these things I saw, and admired the wisdom of God in all His works;"[234] and he himself saw an ox weeping in his stall when his pasture-companion and yoke-fellow was dead.[235] On the other hand, he has "heard from a sailor" about the sea-urchin.

To be sure a great many of the minute observations of creatures and things which Basil records may be discovered by the light of modern science to be incorrect He does not shrink from believing in the spontaneous generation of eels from mud.[236] Yet they stand no less good as proof of his love for God's world of nature, and the reverent enthusiasm and constant delight with which he explored her secrets. His notion of human breathing is that it is the reception of air for the purpose of fanning

---

[233] Hexaem., Hom. v.
[234] Ib. Hom. vii.
[235] Hom. in Mart. Julittam.
[236] Hexaem., vii.

and cooling our internal heat; but he perceives that in
fishes the distension and contraction of the branchiæ,
which take in and discharge the water, discharge the
office of breathing. He notes that there are no mules
among fishes, and that the scarus alone of fishes
ruminates.[237] He tells how gardeners observe a difference
of male and female in their trees, and divide palms into
sexes.[238]

The habits of birds attract his deepest interest; but
though he is perfectly aware that many creatures which
swim are not fish,[239] yet he classes birds according to the
nature of their wings, and places bats and beetles among
them. But he has studied the migrations of some birds:
the love of others for human companionship, the powers
of imitation which others possess. Some of these
creatures are fitted for polity, if it be the proper notion of
polity that the actions of individuals should concur to a
common end. Instance the bees, which Basil imagines to
be governed by a king; "but the king," he remarks, with
a satirical aim at the sovereigns of his own time, "is not
elected by votes, for the ignorance of the multitude has
often raised a most unworthy person to the throne; nor
does he obtain his power by lot, for the chances of the
lot confer principality on the lowest of the low; nor is he
placed on the throne by family succession, for such
persons are apt through indulgence and flattery to be
uninstructed in any virtue. But it is through nature that
he obtains the supremacy, as being the largest and most
beautiful and gentlest of all." And he has observed the
untaught geometry in the construction of the

---

237 Hexaem., Hom. v.
238 Ib. Hom. ix.
239 Ep. clxxxviii.

honeycomb.[240]

"How," he exclaims, "could I recount to you exactly all the peculiarities in the manner of life of various birds; how the cranes set their sentinels by turns at night, and some sleep, while others going the rounds take all care of the slumberers until the end of the watch; and you will observe the same order in their flight." In one of his letters,[241] written in sickness and sorrow, he piteously compares his case with the cranes, as unlike them in his inability to escape the severity of the winter, but too like them in his power to forebode the future. "And the habits of the storks are not far from reason, for at one and the same time they all visit these regions, and at one preconcerted signal they all depart, and our sea-crows act as a body-guard and escort to them, as appears to me, and afford them aid against hostile birds; and the proof of this is, that at that season not a sea-crow is to be seen, and they afterwards return, bringing with them wounds which are plain proofs of the effectual succour they have afforded. Who prescribed to them these laws of alliance? who threatened them with impeachment for desertion, so that none of them fail to do this escort duty?"[242]

Following the lead of a greater preacher than he, Basil derives a multitude of lessons for human life from the habits of the lower creatures. Thus, he applies the conduct of the crows just described as an example of hospitable duty to strangers; and so the gentle behaviour of the storks to their aged would be sufficient to make our children dutiful, would they but attend to the

---

[240] Hexaem., viii. 4.
[241] Ep. cxciii.
[242] Hexaem., Hom. viii.

example.[243] "Let nobody despair on account of his poverty, when he regards the ready resource of the swallow: how in building her nest she carries the straws in her mouth, and, being unable to bring mud with her feet, she moistens with water the extremities of her wings, and, sprinkling them with dust, supplies the want, and binding the straws together with mud, little by little, as with a kind of glue, she brings up her young in the nest."[244]

And yet he is well able to perceive the endowments of the lower creature in which man's intellect finds some dawn or some reflection of itself. "Who is it who announces to the vultures the death of men when they war with one another? For you may see numberless flocks of vultures following the armies, conjecturing from the military preparations what is to follow. This is not far from human reason." Mr. Herbert Spencer, or his interpreter Mr. Fiske, somewhere argues that the operation of mind in the stag, which, from hearing a howl in a thicket, infers the presence of a wild beast, is essentially the same as that of the astronomer, who, from the deflection of a planet in its course infers the existence of an invisible heavenly body beyond it. Basil makes a somewhat similar observation. "The dog, though devoid of reason, has a sense which is of similar power to reason. For what wise men in sedentary lives of much leisure have with difficulty discovered, namely, the connections of the syllogism, this the dog, under the teaching of nature, shows to us. For when he seeks the tracks of wild game, and finding the tracks lead him in many directions, searches first one and then another, does he not by his acts almost speak like our argument

---

[243] Hexaem., Hom. viii.
[244] Ib.

in syllogisms? The beast, he says, is gone either this way or that or that way: now he is not gone that way or that way; it remains that he must be gone this way; and so by exclusion of the false he finds the true.[245]

The bat is both a quadruped and a flying thing; alone of flying things it uses teeth, and brings forth its young like a beast Bats display a mutual love implanted by nature, and hang on to one another like a chain, which is not often the case with men, who for the most part prefer a selfish, separate life to union. How like to owls are the followers of vain wisdom; for as those are sharp-sighted in the darkness but blind in the light, so these have minds very acute in the discovery of vanities, but dim in the perception of true light. The cock should move us by his example to rise early to work. Nor is Basil among those who malign the sense of the goose, that watchful and keenly observant bird which saved the imperial city.[246]

We men remove the old landmarks which our fathers set, and add house to house and field to field, that we may take something from our neighbour; whereas the whales know the manner of life appointed for them by nature, and occupy "that sea without islands beyond the habitable regions of the earth, where no shore lies opposite; wherefore it is untraversed by ships, neither curiosity nor necessity having ever induced sailors to venture it. This sea the whales keep to, resembling in size the largest mountains, as those who have seen them report; observing their own limits, and never troubling either the islands or seaports."[247]

But no sea creature can be compared in remembrance

---

[245] Hexaem., Hom. ix.
[246] Ib. Hom. viii. 7.
[247] Hexaem., vii. 4.

of injuries to the camel, which, when it has been struck treasures up its spite until it can find an opportunity of revenge. Listen to it you who nourish revenge as virtue, and hear what beast you are like.[248] And the changes of the silkworm furnish a striking image of the resurrection, upon which he bids the women meditate as they sit weaving the produce of the silkworm which the Chinese send for the manufacture of soft robes, and not refuse their-faith to that transmutation which Paul announces to mankind.[249]

Sometimes the example of beasts is used with a touch of satire. The craft of the polypus cannot be passed over, which assumes the colour of the rock to which he fixes himself and catches the unwary fish; just like the men who always adapt themselves to the powers that be, and are temperate with the temperate, freelivers with the libertines, whom it is hard to escape, veiling as they do their mischief with an appearance of deep friendship.[250] Again, he tells a wonderful tale how the viper, that venomous reptile, mates with the lamprey, which obeys from the sea the summons of its lover's hiss, just as wives ought to bear with the manners of their husbands, however unpleasing, and on no pretext to seek divorce.[251]

The following observation of the humorous side of natural history was repeated by a mediæval preacher, who illustrates by it the devil's habit of obtaining entrance to hearts by means of little sins. "The crab desires the flesh of the oyster, but the prey is hard to obtain on account of the oyster's shell, whereby nature

---

[248] Id., Hom. viii.
[249] Id. ib.
[250] Id. vii. 3.
[251] Hexaem., Hom. vii. 5.

has protected its soft body. The shells fit accurately, and the crab's claws are necessarily ineffective. What does he do? When he sees the oyster pleasantly sunning himself in some tranquil spot, and opening his valves to receive the sun, then stealthily throwing in a stone he blocks the hinge, and obtains by craft what he never could have got at by strength."[252] The following device of (we believe) the partridge has been lately described by naturalists, who did not know that Basil had been before them:—"I once observed the cunning device of a certain bird: when her young are easily captured by reason of their tender age, she presents herself as an easy prey to the fowlers, and fluttering before them she neither allows herself to be taken, nor deprives them of the hope of capturing her. Thus she affords her young the opportunity of escape, and then she herself flies away. Take heed, lest in like manner you lose the things which you can obtain by grasping at those which you cannot. Come, then, transfer yourself wholly to the Lord, give in your name, enrol yourself in the Church."[253]

His observation on the elephant's trunk might be used by Mr. Darwin. "Because the creature is the vastest of land animals, and formed to strike terror into the beholders, it must needs be furnished with a thick and fleshy body. Now had it been provided with a neck large in proportion to its feet, this neck would have been unmanageable, always bent down by its great weight. But, as it is, the head is united to the spine by a few vertebræ, and it has a trunk which answers the purpose of a neck, by means of which it obtains its food and drink."[254]

---

[252] Hexaem., Hom. vii. 5.
[253] Hom. in Sanct. Bapt.
[254] Hexaem., Hom. ix.

It would not be easy to find any wholly fabulous creature alluded to by Basil except the beautiful sailors' fancy of the halcyon, "which lays its eggs in the sand hard by the sea, and hatches them in winter when the waves beat hardest against the shore. But the winds all sleep, and the waves are at rest for seven days, while the halcyon sits upon her eggs. And when the young ones come to need their food, then the beneficent God allows seven days more for the growth of this minute creature. And the sailors are aware of this, and call these the halcyon days. And care for the brute creatures is ordained by God, that you may be encouraged to ask of God what you need for your salvation."[255]

But, he exclaims, "I should be as unable to express in words all the wonders of flying creatures as to come up with their speed upon my feet."[256] "Let the man who thinks he can attain to the knowledge of existences explain to me the nature of the smallest creature which is, and tell me the constitution of the ant; if its life is maintained by breathing; if its body possesses bones; if it is strung with nerves and sinews; if its nerves are kept in place by muscles and glands; if its marrow extends through the vertebræ of the spine from head to tail; he that boasts of his knowledge let him explain the ant, then let him come to explain the nature of Him who passeth all understanding. But if thou hast not yet grasped in knowledge the little ant, how dost thou boast that thou canst image to thyself the imcomprehensible power of God?"

"Regard the form of quadrupeds, how their heads are bent towards the earth. Thy head is raised towards heaven. Thine eyes behold the things above, so that if

[255] Hexaem., viii. 5.
[256] Hexaem., viii.

ever thou dost dishonour thyself by the lusts of the flesh, serving sensuality and gluttony, thou art compared unto the beasts that perish. Another care becomes thee, to seek those things which are above, and to be in thought above earthly things. As thou art formed so dispose thy life. Have thy citizenship in the heavens. Jerusalem above is thy true native land; thy fellow-citizens and fellow-tribesmen are the firstborn, whose names are written in heaven."[257]

---

[257] Hexaem., ix. 2.

CHAPTER XIV
The Preacher

St. Basil possessed every endowment which is needed for a great preacher. Words at will, ample stores of thought and knowledge, a striking presence, and the orator's ambition to influence men, purged of all selfish taint by the inspirations of faith and love. It is hard to see how he could have failed, except through want of physical strength to make his voice heard, or through the entire absence of a sympathetic audience. We do find him complaining that he cannot finish his address, since his voice fails through his life-long infirmity. He will finish it the next day, unless he is reduced to total silence.[258] He compares his own weakness and his hearers' eagerness to a poor mother trying in vain to supply the wants of a lusty infant.[259] But his weakness was habitually overcome by his energy and zeal; a victory over self, the sight of which is in itself a source of power over a sensitive audience.

And the quick-witted, excitable Greeks among whom he lived furnished him with congregations which,

---

[258] Hom. in Ps. i.
[259] Hom. in Ps. lix.

however hard it might be to affect them permanently, were for the time all that an orator could desire. What would not a modern preacher give to be listened to by the class of hearers whom he had? "I do not forget that many artisans of the manufacturing classes stand around me, who, scarcely earning their bread by their day's labour, compel me to shorten my discourse that they may not be kept for long from their work." Yet these were sermons preached every morning and evening during the season of Lent, and he expected his working men to return to him again in the same day. He therefore affords them opportunity to dispose of their business during the intervening time, and return with minds purged from care to their repast of the evening's discourse.[260] And then he hopes that they will make what they have heard the subject of their conversation at supper.[261]

At other times they displayed more embarrassing signs of their interest in sermons. In preaching on the creation, he had in the heat of his discourse at first forgotten the birds; and he tells us how he was reminded of them. "Some may wonder why I have just made a considerable pause in my sermon, but my more attentive hearers know the reason of it; those, namely, who, by their looks at one another and their signs, have called my attention to them and brought back my thoughts to what I had omitted."[262] And on another occasion: "I perceive long ago that you are discontented with my sermon, and I almost hear you saying that I am spending my time upon points which are admitted, and avoiding to touch upon burning questions. For now the

---

[260] Hexaem., Hom. iii.
[261] Ib. Hom. vii.
[262] Ib. Hom. viii.

ears of all are erect to hear something on the doctrine of the Holy Spirit."[263] And again, some brethren who are standing by suggest to him that he ought not to omit noticing a fire which had taken place on the previous day, providentially sparing the church.[264]

It would seem from these last quotations that the sermons of St. Basil were extempore. And we might adduce other phrases which go to prove the same. "What comes into my mind in speaking" must not be omitted. Yet this latter phrase is capable of the explanation that to say what only came into his mind at the time must have been exceptional, and that his sermons were very carefully prepared beforehand. We know from Gregory of Nazianzus that shorthand writers were employed at the time to take down sermons, and some of St. Basil's may have come to us direct from their notes. But others are too finished to allow us to doubt that, like other great orators of antiquity, he wrote them out carefully after delivery, if not before it.

There is one of Basil's sermons[265] which is noted in an ancient MS. as having been preached while he was still a deacon. And we can trace a very marked difference between its character and that of nearly all the rest. It is a theme or exercise, thoughtful and ingenious, but without much life or force. The sermons of after-times, when the saint has acquired larger experience of men and has got well into his work, are of quite another character. They are eminently living and sympathetic. Although the requirements of self-denial which they make are very high, and neither rich nor poor are spared, yet the arguments used and the point of view in

---

[263] Hom. contr. Sabell.
[264] Hom. Quod non mundanis adhær.
[265] Hom. xii. in princip. Proverb.

which duties are set often surprise us by their pliant adaptation to the minds addressed. There have been ascetics who cried in the wilderness and were reverenced from a distance by the every-day world, which at the same time felt no common ground with them and never thought of practising what they taught. But Basil, thorough ascetic as he was, presents to us in his dealing with souls no such aspect as this. While we read his ascetic works it seems to us that he must have regarded the outward world as well-nigh handed over to Satan. Again and again it is argued with merciless force that to break one least command of God is to break the whole law. Every counsel of perfection is to be practised for the very saving of the soul. In the sermons to the people we do not indeed find the asceticism forgotten, but we find the utmost charity and allowance, a practical instinct which puts things in the light most likely to be effective, a knowledge of the profane world and its ways, which we scarcely know how such a man can have come by. Probably it will be felt that this severity, on the one hand, to self, and to those who occupy the same position with oneself, and this wide charity on the other, which works in the world without despair or aversion, is far from being inconsistent with the spirit of New Testament Christianity. At all events, that is what we find in our saint.

For instance, we find two sermons on Fasting at the commencement of the collection. In the first place, nobody should be grim and sad while fasting. It is for our spiritual good, and it is absurd to be sorrowful over a change of food while the soul is being cured. The principle of fasting lies in the primitive command, "Thou shalt not eat of it." Do not speak to me of bodily weakness or inability. You cannot fast, say you, and yet you can all your life be eating to satiety. Why, it is not variety of meats but restraint in food that physicians are always prescribing; and if you are able to bear the variety, how can you plead that you are not equal to the restraint? Read the fate of the rich man, who, not for any crime, but for softness of life, was tormented in the flame. Take care lest you who now despise water should hereafter, like that rich man, crave a drop. Nobody ever had a headache through water-drinking. Nobody ever lost the proper use of his feet or of his hands through irrigating them with water. Let the knife of your cook have some rest, and your table be content with what grows of itself. Let the fast be a Sabbath of rest to your servants, who minister to you unceasingly all through the year. Give repose to your cook and leisure to the decorator of your table; stay the hand of your winebearer. Let the house for once enjoy silence from the numberless noises and the smoke and the savour and the constant running up and down of those who have to pay their service to the stomach as if to an imperious mistress.

The most popular species of discourse seems to have been that pronounced upon the festival of a martyr, when bishops from other churches were wont to attend and grace the services. The people were never weary of hearing the story and the eulogy of the local saints. Nevertheless, it does not seem to us that Basil's sermons, produced to order, as it were, for such occasions, though they are elaborate, are by any means his grandest efforts. And perhaps they were not the subjects he most enjoyed, for we find him using the excuse that his sermon of the previous day was left unfinished, to pass from the subject of the martyr, Julitta, and treat the text "in everything give thanks."

The subject on which Basil is sure to put forth all his powers is that of charity, and the duty of the rich to the poor. " 'What shall I do?' says the rich man in the parable. Who would not pity a man so beset? Pitiable for his abundance, wretched for his good things present, more wretched still on account of what awaits him. His land brings him not produce, but sighs. He does not lay up for himself fruits, but care, and sorrow, and grievous anxiety. He laments like the poor. Is it not the very same thing that the poverty-stricken man says? What shall I do? Where shall I find food or raiment? What shall I do? You might well have said, I will fill the soul of the hungry. I will open my barns and summon all who are in need. I will imitate Joseph, and cry with a loud voice, All you in want of bread, come to me, and each one take his fill from the gracious gifts of God, as if from a common fountain. Soul, thou hast much goods laid up: eat, drink, and be merry. What madness! If thou hadst a swine's soul, what else wouldst thou say to it but this. How thankful oughtest thou be to the Bountiful one, how joyful for the honour given thee, that thou dost not crowd the door of other men, but others occupy thine! But now thou art morose, and avoidest meeting the poor, lest, perhaps, thou be compelled to give something. One reply alone thou knowest how to give: I cannot, I will not give. I am poor. Yes, truly poor thou art, and in need of all things. Poor in love, poor in kindness, poor in faith toward God, poor in eternal hope."[266]

"The young man who came asking, Good master, what shall I do? displays to us a mingled character. For to have known the true Master, and passing by the pride

---

[266] Hom. in illud Lucæ, destruam horrea.

of the Pharisees, and the self-opinion of the lawyers, and the vanity of the scribes, to have made his request to the one true Master, this was praiseworthy; and again, to have shown himself so anxious to obtain eternal life. But this is what convicts him of inconsistency and want of harmony within himself: you call Him master, yet you will not do the part of disciples. You confess Him good, yet you reject His gifts. And yet what hard thing was it that He asked of thee? Sell what thou hast and give to the poor. Had he proposed to thee work in the fields, or the perils of the merchantman, or any of the other toilsome labours which men submit to in pursuit of gain, thou mightest well have been sad; but when He promises to make thee heir of eternal life in a way so easy, involving neither toil nor sweat, thou dost not rejoice at the easiness of salvation, but goest away sorrowful.… What befell this young man and others like him, resembles, to my thinking, the case of some traveller who, though longing to see a certain city, should, with toil and pain, accomplish the journey thither, and putting up at an inn outside the walls should, through indolent dislike of exertion, render useless all his previous labour, and deprive himself of the sight of all the wonders of the place. Such are they who willingly fulfil all the other commandments, but shrink from depriving themselves of their wealth. I know many persons who fast, pray, groan, and display every act of religion that costs nothing, but will not spend a penny upon the poor. But you say, After having enjoyed my property during my life, I shall make the poor the heirs of it by will. That is to say, when you are no longer among men, then you will become kind to men; when I see you dead, then I am to call you loving to your brethren. Much thanks will be due to you for your generosity when, being laid in the tomb and turned to dust, you become lavish and magnanimous in expending your wealth. Tell me, pray, for which period is it that you ask to be rewarded; for your lifetime or the time after your death? But while you were alive you would not in your luxury cast a look at the poor. And after death what action can there be; what reward is there to be earned? Show the work and demand the recompense. No one does business when the market is over; no one is crowned who comes when the race is done; no one gains fame after the war is past; and after life there is no cultivating virtue…. But why do you wait for a time in which often people are not even master of their own intellects? It will be the dead of night and your sickness will be heavy, and no one to help you; and somebody scheming for your inheritance will be ready to manage everything for his own advantage and disappoint your purposes. Then you will look this way and that, and see the solitude that surrounds you and understand your madness; then will you lament the folly which put off keeping the commandment to such a time as this, when the paralysed tongue and the trembling hand, already contracted by the death-throes, shall leave you neither voice nor sign to make your wishes known. And though all were clearly set down and every word plainly spoken, yet one letter inserted might change the whole disposition; one counterfeit seal, two or three false witnesses, might transfer the whole inheritance to another."

There happened, during Basil's ministry, a frightful famine, and we have his sermon preached during its prevalence to move to charity his "children whom he had begotten in the Gospel and tended as infants by the benediction of his hands." "A cloudless sky above the

earth which is dried up, barren and fruitless, scored with
fissures, the sun's rays piercing its recesses. Our rich
perennial fountains have failed us, and our rivers are
dried up, so that little children and women with burdens
can step over them.… Reapers there are many, but no
harvest. The husbandmen sitting in the fields embracing
their knees with their hands, as mourners are wont to
do, deplore their vain toil, look upon their young
children and lament, gaze upon their wives and weep,
touch and handle the scorched grass, and groan aloud as
fathers who have lost their sons.… What prayers, then,
and supplications are we offering? You men, except a
few, occupy yourselves in your business; you women
minister to the men in the works of mammon. Few are
with me at prayers, and these giddy and yawning,
constantly turning their heads and waiting for the cantor
to have finished the psalms, when, as from a prison,
they will be delivered from the church and from the task
of prayer. And these little boys, who leave their copy
tablets in the school and uplift their voices with us,
rather take part in the work as a relaxation and a
pleasure, regarding our mourning as a holiday, since
they are set free for a while from the fear of the master
and the care of learning. But the multitude of grown-up
men, and the people habituated to sin, wander through
the city, careless, thoughtless, and gay; though they be
the ones who bear about in their souls that which has
brought the calamity upon us. Simple and guileless
children gather together and come to our services of
confession, though they be neither the cause of the
calamity, nor have the knowledge or capacity for
habitual prayer.… Listen, Christian people. Thus saith
the Lord, not by His own mouth indeed, but using those
of His servants as His instruments. Let not us who are

endowed with reason seem more cruel than the brutes.
For they use in common the produce of the earth. The
flocks of sheep feed on the same mountain-side: the
horses in the same plain. But we hide in our bosoms the
possessions that ought to be common, and keep alone
what belongs to many. Let us take shame to hear what is
told of the humanity of heathen Greeks. Among some of
them there was a common table, common food, a single
family composed of a numerous people. Or come we to
the example of the three thousand; and imitate the first
Christian assembly, who had all things common, life,
soul, and love, a common table, a close brotherhood, an
unfeigned love, many bodies busied about the same
object, and different souls attuned to one harmony....
Perchance, avarice tempts you, as Potiphar's wife did
Joseph, but cast away your garments and flee. Keep
your faith to God as he did to his master. Provide for the
famine but for one year, as he did for seven. Give not all
to pleasure; give something to your soul. Think that you
have two daughters—the prosperity of this life and the
happiness of heaven. If thou wilt not give all to the
better, divide, at least, your property between the
dissolute daughter and the modest. When you come to
stand before Christ, and arrive in the presence of your
Judge, exhibit not to Him this life enriched beyond
measure, and the other covered with rags, to be His
bride.... These things are no fables, but truth proclaimed
by the voice that could not lie. And know assuredly that,
according to the declaration of the Lord, one jot or one
tittle shall in no wise pass away. But the body which
mouldered in the tomb shall rise, and the same soul
which was separated by death shall dwell in it again.
And a clear record of our life will be produced not by
external witnesses, but by the testimony of our own

consciences. And the just Judge will render to each according to his works; to whom is due glory and power and adoration for ever and ever. Amen."

We can well imagine the effect of words like these from a man who, in this same famine, had distributed among the starving the last farthing of his earthly possessions. But surely a strange picture of the littleness of life while it is passing, compared with its greatness when well passed, is afforded by the great saint and doctor of the Church conducting his special famine services with none to join him except a few yawning people and little boys sent up to church from the school.

CHAPTER XV
Eloquence

The eloquence of St. Basil is agreed by all competent judges to be not unworthy of comparison with that of the Greek orators of the best period. Erasmus, Fénélon, Bossuet, Villemain, themselves masters in the science of expression, have paid their homage to him; and, in truth, the eloquence of Basil possesses something which even the Attic could not attain to. He is as thoroughly in earnest as Demosthenes pleading for his country; but even the love of country could not furnish Demosthenes with such lofty themes as the salvation of souls and the infinite love of God. Moreover, there was an element of culture in Basil which the Athenian wanted; namely, the Bible. The character of the oratory of our saint is recognized to consist in this union of the Oriental eloquence of Scripture with the Greek, to which he was natural heir. This union may sometimes produce passages which seem a little turgid to a taste formed as ours is so much upon the eloquence of debaters. Yet Basil never can be accused of making ornament a purpose. We learn from Gregory Nyssen that his style was sometimes regarded as over simple. No passage can

be produced from him that displays the same
consciousness of his own powers which his friend
Gregory Nazianzen naïvely expresses. He never loses
sight of his object, and his speaking and writing
everywhere show the distinctive faculty of eloquence. If
we mistake not, that which forces from most men the
confession that they have been listening to eloquence, is
not merely a power of clear narrative or convincing
argument. It is the power which consists in impressing a
great central idea, perhaps an old and hackneyed one,
compelling the mind to rest on it without fatigue or
sense of sameness, and contemplate it in various points
of view, amid every association of charm and of force
which can be imparted by illustrative argument, wit,
graphic power, and sustained loftiness of sentiment: and
all this with unstrained ease and mastery.

Mere extracts, even if our limits allowed of extensive
ones, cannot do justice to an orator so eminently
connected and continuous as Basil. But we shall try to
select two or three passages which it is possible to
separate.

" 'Let the earth bring forth.' Conceive the cold and
childless earth upon that brief command at once in
labour, and moved to bring forth fruit, casting off, as it
were, her sullen and mournful garb, clad instead with a
gay robe, rejoicing in ornaments of her own production,
and yielding the infinite varieties of growing things. I
would that the wonder of creation should be deeply
fixed in your mind, that wherever you find yourself, and
by whatever species of plant you stand, you may receive
a clear reminder of the Maker of all. When you see the
grass and its flower, think of the nature of man, and
remember the image of the wise Isaiah—'All flesh is as
grass, and all the glory of man as the flower of grass.'

For the shortness of life, and the charm and gaiety of human happiness, so soon over, are thus most fitly imaged by the prophet. To-day flourishing in health of body, high fed and ruddy, in the flower of age, full and well knit, and irresistible in energy; to-morrow, miserable, withered by time or exhausted by disease. One man is conspicuous for the multitude of his riches; a crowd of flatterers surround him; an escort of pretended friends seek his favour; a crowd of relations skilled in the courtier's arts, an innumerable band of followers, besiege him, to furnish some his food, others every other need; and when he goes and comes with such a train, he arouses the envy of the beholders. Add also to his wealth some political office, some honour from the prince, either the government of nations or the command of armies; a herald crying with loud voice before him, lictors on this side and on that, bringing abject terror to the governed, with stripes, confiscation of goods, exile, prison; intolerable fear of him is diffused among his subjects. And what follows? One night, a fever, a pleurisy, an inflammation of the lungs, carries him off from among men, strips of a sudden all the stage, and his glory stands convicted of being but a dream."[267]

"Life is called the way, because that every one who lives is pressing on towards the end. For as they that sleep on ship-board are carried on without effort of theirs by the winds and waves, and though they themselves perceive it not, their voyage hastens on to its close; so we, as the period of our life flows by, are carried forward as with a constant and unceasing motion, by the unmarked lapse of life, each one to his

---

[267] Hexaem., Hom. v.

own appointed end. For example, you sleep, the time runs by; you waken and are occupied in thought, time is spending, though it escape our perception. All men run a race which carries each one forward, pressing on every one to his own goal: and so we are all on the way. And thus you may conceive the idea of the way. You are a traveller in this life. Everything passes by, and falls behind you. Plant, or herb, or stream, or whatever else you see worth notice by the way, delights for a little while, and then you pass on. Again, you happen upon stones, upon ruts, upon precipices, rocks, stakes, or even upon wild beasts, reptiles, thorns, and other dangers; you are troubled for a little while, and then pass on. Such is life, possessing neither abiding joys nor unchanging grief. The way is not thine, nor do the things that are present belong to thee, just as when the first traveller lifts his foot, the second plants his upon the spot, and after him the next."[268]

Libanius, if the letters to Basil in his name be genuine, requests a sight of the homily upon drunkenness; and whether the utterance of Libanius or not, the request stands good as a proof that this homily was thought at the time a powerful effort of Basil's eloquence. We subjoin a portion of it, more especially as it gives a strange picture of the morals of the period.

"The scenes which I beheld yesterday evening move me to speak; but on the other hand this impulse is restrained and my eagerness repressed by the fruitlessness of my past labours. A husbandman, if the first seed has not sprung up, is slow to scatter seed again upon the same field. For if from so many exhortations which I addressed to you, as well in past times as

---

afterwards during the seven weeks of Lent, in which
night and day I preached to you the gospel of the grace
of God, no fruit and no use has come, with what hope
can I speak to you to-day? Alas! how many nights did
you keep vigil in vain? and how many days did you
assemble in vain, if it be indeed in vain?

"A single evening, a single assault of the enemy, has
dissipated all my toil. What desire can I have, then, to
speak? I should have kept silence, be assured of it, had I
not feared the example of Jeremiah, who, when he
shrank from speaking to an unbelieving people, suffered
what he himself has told us. For the word of the Lord
was unto him as a burning fire shut up in his bones, and
he was weary with forbearing and he could not stay....
Dissolute women, forgetting the fear of God, despising
the everlasting fire, on a day when they should have
remained at home to remember the resurrection and to
take thought of that day when the heavens shall be
opened and our Judge shall appear from heaven, and of
God's trumpets, and of the resurrection of the dead, and
the just judgment, and the retribution to every one
according to his works—instead of having these things
in their thoughts, and purging their hearts from evil
desires, and washing their past sins away with tears, and
making ready to meet Christ at the great day of His
appearing—they shook off the yoke of Christ's service,
they tore from their heads the veil of modesty, they
despised God and His angels,[269] they shamelessly faced
the gaze of every male, shook out their hair, trailed their
tunics, and with tripping feet, with wanton eyes, and
peals of laughter, dancing like Bacchanals, inviting all
the licentiousness of young men, arranged their dances

____

[269] This passage shows us what was Basil's interpretation of 1 Cor. 11:10.

in the very churches of the martyrs before the city walls and made the holy places themselves the workshops of their impurity. They defiled the air with their harlot songs, they defiled the ground with their unclean feet as they trod it in their dance, making themselves a spectacle to the young men standing round, utterly immodest and frantic, and leaving unpractised no species of madness.[270] How can I keep silence about such things? How can I lament them enough? It is wine that has wrought for us the destruction of these souls; wine, which was given by God to the sober for a help to infirmity, but now is made by the intemperate an instrument of excess."

"Drunkenness, that self-chosen devil, taking possession of the mind through pleasure: drunkenness, the parent of sin, the enemy of virtue, makes the brave man a coward, the chaste vicious; it knows no righteousness: it casts away prudence. I am slow to attack drunkenness, not because it is a slight evil, but because all I say is likely to have little effect. For if the drunkard is out of his senses, in vain you chide one who hears you not. Whom shall I address? If it is those who want the admonition, they cannot listen to what I say, and if it is the temperate and sober, they do not require my words. Perhaps, then, as in times of pestilence, physicians, though they may not help those who are diseased, are wont to fortify the healthy with some preventive medicines; so my discourse may be partly useful in supplying a protection and an antidote to the healthy, though not freedom or cure to the victims.

"How do you differ, O man, from the brutes? Is it

---

[270] That such drunken scenes were not peculiar to Asia Miner may be judged by the fact that St. Ambrose borrowed for sermons a considerable part of the present discourse, including the foregoing passage.

not in the gift of reason, by the reception whereof from
your Creator you were made chief and lord of all the
creatures? Whoever, therefore, by drunkenness deprives
himself of his reason, is compared unto the beasts that
perish. Rather would I say that the drunkard is more
void of reason than the beasts … For what brute animal
is so dull in the sense of hearing and of seeing as
drunkards? They know not their own friends, and run to
strangers as if they were their nearest and dearest, and
jump over shadows, mistaking them for rivulets or clefts
in the ground? Their ears are filled with a sound like the
roaring of the sea. The ground seems to rise up and the
mountains to whirl Sometimes they laugh incessantly
and sometimes lament inconsolably. Sometimes they are
bold and rash, and sometimes trembling and fearful
Their sleep is dull and hard to shake off, and so heavy as
to border on death; their waking more stupid than sleep;
for their life is a dream. Who, though they have neither
garment nor food for the morrow, are kings and
commanders of armies in their drink, construct cities,
and scatter money; with such visions and delusions does
wine fill their heart. While others fall into the opposite
extreme and are doleful, tearful, and a prey to terrors.…
Their eyes are bloodshot; their skin is yellow; their
intelligence languid; their tongue hesitating; their voice
harsh; their feet unsteady like those of little children …
And they compound drugs to aid their drunkenness; not
to hinder them from suffering evil from it, but to enable
them to be perpetually and without intermission drunk.
The day is too short, even the winter nights too brief for
them, as affording time for drinking. And there is no end
to the evil. For the drink urges them on to require more.
It does not relieve their craving, but induces an
inevitable necessity for drinking again, inflaming the

intoxicated and always provoking the desire to drink. But while they aim at maintaining a continual thirst, it falls out otherwise than they intended. For by the constant enjoyment they render their sense of taste dull and languid…. 'Who hath woe? who hath sorrow? who hath contentions? who hath babbling? who hath wounds without cause? who hath redness of eyes? They that tarry long at the wine. They that go to seek mixed wine.' Worthy of lamentation are they, for 'drunkards shall not inherit the kingdom of God.' … And what human constitution is strong enough to withstand the evils of drink? By what arts can it be brought about that the body always heated, always soaked in wine, shall not become weak and a prey to fluxes. Hence tremblings and debility; for through immoderate use of wine the breath becomes short and broken, the strength of the nerves relaxed; agitation and tremor of the whole frame ensue. Why do you desire to draw down on yourself the curse of Cain, trembling and wandering through your life?

"How long is this drunkenness to last? You are in danger of turning at last into mud, instead of man, so mixed with liquor you are, you and it becoming corrupted together, smelling of stale drink, like vessels fit for no use. Such does Isaiah lament over. 'Woe to them that arise in the morning to follow strong drink, and continue until night till wine inflame them.' … Those who in the beginning of the day search for places where to hold their revels, and haunt the wine-shops and taverns, and meet together to drink, and devote all their care to this—these does the prophet grieve for, because they leave themselves no time to regard the wonderful works of God. Their eyes have no leisure to look up to heaven and learn its beauty, and view the fair order of

created things, thereby to comprehend the Maker of
them; and he among them who drinks most carries off
the victory from the rest. Truly their glory is in their
shame. They vie with one another, and they avenge
each other upon themselves. What words can tell the
shame of what is done? All is full of madness, all of
confusion; the defeated are drank, and the victors are
drunk; the attendants mock them; their hands lose their
power; their mouths will not retain what is put in them;
the wretched body, deprived of its natural vigour, is
utterly relaxed, unable to resist the violence of excess....
A miserable spectacle for the eyes of Christian men. A
man in the flower of his years, strong in frame,
distinguished in the ranks of the army, is carried home
by others, because he cannot get up and walk away
upon his own feet: a man who ought to be a terror to the
enemy is the laughing-stock of boys in the market-place;
he is prostrated without a weapon, he is slain without a
foe. A man of arms, in the very flower of his age, is
conquered by wine, and ready to suffer whatever his
enemies desire to inflict. Drunkenness is the bane of
reason, the destruction of vigour; it is premature age; it
is death before the time. How like are drunkards to the
idols of the Gentiles, which have eyes, and see not; ears
have they, and hear not: their hands are useless, their
feet paralysed. Who can have devised such a thing?
Who can have inflicted such evil? Who can have
mingled for us this cup of madness? O man, it is not a
banquet thou hast prepared, but an embattled army!
Thou castest forth the young men, led away like
wounded from a battle; thou hast slain the vigour of
their youth with wine, and thou callest one in to supper
as a friend, and after throwest him out like one dead
when thou hast extinguished the life in him by wine.

And when they might seem to be full enough of wine, then, forsooth, it is that they begin to drink; and drink they do, like a beast out of a perennial fountain supplying spouts equal in number to the boon companions. For, as the banquet proceeds, a young man enters, broad-shouldered and strong, and not yet drunk, bearing a mighty jar of cool wine. He thrusts aside their cup-bearers, and, standing in the middle, he distributes through curved tubes to each an equal share of drunkenness. A new fashion this of measuring what has no measure, so that they may commit their excess with strict fairness, and none may get the better of the other. For, taking possession each of the tube opposite to him, they drink at one breath, like oxen out of the same pond, striving to draw into their throats as much as the wine-cooler above lets down to them through its silver spouts.… Woe to them that rise in the morning to follow strong drink, that continue until night till wine inflame them. The heat of the wine communicating itself to their flesh becomes a match to light the fiery darts of the enemy: for wine drowns the reason and the mind, and rouses the passions like a swarm of bees. What chariot dragged by steeds is hurried on so headlong when the charioteer has been thrown? What ship without a steersman, borne hither and thither by the waves, is not safer than the drunken man?

"Through these mischiefs men, ay and women too, join in the dance, and deliver up their souls to the demon of wine. Laughter rises on every side, and shameful songs. Do you laugh? Do you rejoice with a disgraceful joy when you ought to be lamenting for the sins which have overtaken you? Do you sing profane songs, forgetting the psalms and hymns which you had learned? Do you move your feet, and bound like one

mad, and dance as you ought never to dance, when you
should bend your knees to worship? Which shall I
sorrow for most: the unwedded virgins, or those already
married, who, even if they have escaped actual sin, yet
have imbibed corruption in their souls?… Alas! how will
Pentecost receive you who have thus insulted Easter? At
Pentecost the descent of the Holy Spirit was manifested
to all men, but you in anticipation have made yourself
the dwelling of the ghostly enemy, and have become the
temple of idols, when you should have become, by the
indwelling of the Holy Ghost, the temple of God. You
have invoked upon yourself the curse of the prophet,
who says in the person of God, 'will turn your feasts
into mourning.' How will you command your servants,
when you, like bond-slaves, are the servants of foolish
and hurtful lusts? How will you chasten your children
while you live an unchastened and unregulated life?
What, then? shall I leave you thus? I fear lest the sinner
become more disobedient, and the repentant be
swallowed up with overmuch sorrow. Let abstinence be
the cure for drunkenness, psalms for shameful songs,
tears for laughter. Instead of dancing, let the knee be
bent; instead of clapping of hands, beat your breasts;
instead of costly raiment, show humility, and especially
let alms be thy rescue from sin, for the ransom of a
man's life are his riches. Engage many of the afflicted to
be the helpers of thy prayers, if perchance the thought of
thy heart may be forgiven thee. When the people sat
down to eat and drink, and rose up to play (but idolatry
was their play), then the Levites, arming themselves
against their brethren, consecrated their hands to the
priesthood. To you, then, who fear the Lord, and who
now have sorrowed over the shame of these disgraceful
acts, I give this charge: if you see any repentant over the

folly of their deeds, feel for them as for your own
members; but if you see them obstinate, and despising
your grief for them, come out from among them, and be
ye separate, and touch not the unclean thing, that so
they may be visited with shame, and come to the
knowledge of their own sinfulness, and you may receive
the reward of the zeal of Phinehas, through the just
judgment of our God and Saviour Jesus Christ, to
whom be glory and power for ever and ever. Amen."

CHAPTER XVI
The Classical Scholar

We have seen how thorough had been Basil's education in the best secular learning of his time. Even had the records of his life been lost, his works would have sufficed to prove the depth of his classical culture, for there is none of the fathers who makes so much use of heathen authors. When it falls to his lot to write to men of the world, we nearly always find the letter full of classical allusions. He has to reply to a letter of Candidianus, and make interest with him to procure redress for an impudent outrage committed upon his house at Annesi. His epistle tells how he has opened the letter of Candidianus with as much trepidation as an accused Spartan a despatch from the government. But agreeably surprised by the easy method of the great man's address, he gives him the advantage over Demosthenes, who, when he had furnished forth a choir, demanded that he should be called, not Demosthenes, but the choragos, while Candidianus, in command of many thousand soldiers, is the same Candidianus to his friends as ever. He resembles Plato, who, amidst the storm and stress of business, can retire in spirit to the shelter of a strong wall and be disturbed by none of it.[271]

Basil begs the intercession of Martinianus with the Emperor, piteously describing the injury which Cæsarea has received from the division of the province of Cappadocia. The letter serves to show not only his readiness of classical allusion, but his interest in the general culture of his town. According to custom, the great man is propitiated with a compliment, that to have met him is better than to have seen, like Ulysses, the manners and cities of many men. And while Alcinous would have liked to listen to Ulysses for a year, Basil would wish the company of his accomplished friend for a lifetime. Such were the elaborate compliments which then took the place of our shorter, but not more sincere, Dear Sir. The present cause of his writing is the calamity of his afflicted country, torn in pieces like Pentheus by the Mænads. Would that he had the pen of a Simonides to describe its woe; nay, why Simonides? rather Æschylus, or some author with his skill for the moving description of sorrow. All those pleasant assemblages and conversations of learned persons in the market-place of Cæsarea have passed away. It is more rare to meet a man of culture there than it used to be to meet in the Athenian assembly a man branded with public infamy. And in the place of culture has come the rudeness of barbarians. The only sounds heard are the voices of those demanding dues, or of those replying to such demands, or of those suffering under the lash. The porticoes on every side render a gloomy sound as though the echoes uttered a voice of their own, lamenting the sad case. Our anxiety about our very life

---

[271] Ep. iii.

hinders our lamenting as we should otherwise do the shutting up of our gymnasia, and our streets without light. And there seems the greatest danger of the total desertion of our town by the best portion of its aristocracy. Will not Martinianus do something, or, if he is powerless, at least behave like Solon, who, when he found himself unable to defend his fellow citizens, sat armed before his door, to show at least that he was no party to what was done?[272]

Basil writes to Diodorus of Antioch that he has perused a work which the latter had sent him. He finds its brevity very acceptable, old and weak as he now is; and the directness of the reasoning appears to him very worthy of a Christian writer, who ought to work, not for ostentation, but for the common utility. But as for the abuse of adversaries and laudations of friends which are intermingled; though such figures of speech may seem to adorn the composition, yet he thinks they only divert the mind from the argument. And he reminds his correspondent that Aristotle and Theophrastus, conscious of their deficiency in Plato's grace of style, proceed straight to the matter in hand, while such is Plato's power, that he can at the same time attack his adversary's argument, and hit off his personal peculiarities in true dramatic fashion, as, *e.g.* the levity of a Hippias, the arrogance of a Protagorus, the rashness and impudence of a Thrasymachus. But where he introduces undefined interlocutors in his dialogues, he uses them merely for the sake of perspicuity, but mingles nothing personal in the argument, as in the "De Legibus." And the same course is very fitting for us, even if it be worth our while at all to leave our subject

---

[272] Ep. lxxiv.

for the sake of attacking persons. These observations seem to prove that Basil knew his Plato and Aristotle, and was a candid and valuable critic as well.[273]

But, indeed, there is abundance of proof from many parts of his works that he had been a close student of Aristotle. We have already remarked that he makes great use of the natural history of that author, and his ethical works are among the models and materials of Basil's thought: instance the early lecture on the beginning of the Book of Proverbs, which is full of Aristotelian expressions and modes of thinking. Another favourite author was Plutarch. M. Fialon, in an interesting chapter of his study on St. Basil, gives us in parallel columns some portions of a sermon of the Saint, with the original passages in Plutarch from which they are derived. In using them, the great orator proves at the same time his own original genius, and his familiarity with the heathen moralist, by the ease with which he adapts the borrowed materials to his own purpose, enforcing them with apposite quotations from Scripture, and filling them not only with Christian spirit, but with new vividness and force. A still more important influence was exercised over our saint by the Neo-Platonic school of philosophy; for to it he resorts, not merely for observations of nature and mankind, but for theology. The doctrine of Plotinus includes a supreme principle, perfect and one; Being without qualities, the source of all and everything; also a Demiurge, or active and creative power, co-operating with the first, and a Soul or influence shed from the Demiurge among the creatures. And this system had so great authority with Basil that a sermon by him upon the Holy Spirit, and a

---

[273] Ep. cxxxv.

whole chapter of his theological treatise on the same subject, are centos from the works of Plotinus.[274]

Among the homilies is one addressed to young men upon the use to be made of the works of Gentile authors. It is very full of kindliness and wisdom, and forms a good example of the flexibility of mind by which Basil, ascetic though he was, could throw himself with sympathy into the feelings of those whom a narrow spirit or an attempt at dictation would doubtless have repelled, as it does the youth of our own day. He claims the right to address them conferred upon him by his age and the many experiences of his eventful life, and a loving care for their interests second only to that of their parents.

It seems as though the youthful intellect of that day found in the pleasant haunts of classical literature a refuge from the controversies of theology, much as that of our time does in science or literary culture. For Basil seems all along to found his appeal to them upon the basis that what he desires of them is in truth consonant with the best mind of the poets and philosophers. And he begins by hoping that they will be able to claim the second place in Hesiod's classification, who sets first those who of themselves know what is right, and second those who are able to follow the good advice of others. He asks of them then that they should not commit the entire guidance of their lives to heathen teachers, but take from them what is good and leave what ought to be rejected. The use of a tree is to produce fruit, but the leaves as they wave add beauty; just so, the fruit of the soul is *truth;* and yet a clothing of external wisdom is not ungrateful as affording a shadow and an ornament to

---

[274] Fialon. Étude sur St. Basile, pp. 244, 245.

truth.

When, therefore, the poets tell us of the words and deeds of the good, let us love and follow their lessons; but when they tell us of evil, let us stop our ears, like Ulysses at the song of the Syrens. To become habituated to hear what is evil is to be on the way to acts of evil. Poison may be taken mixed with honey; and we will not praise the poets when they revile other people or when they mock; when they depict sensual love or drinking; when they measure happiness by the full table and the dissolute song; least of all when they teach divinity. Let us try to take the best they have to give; let us visit them like the bees, who not merely enjoy scent and colour in the flowers as others do, but gather honey. They rest not on every flower, nor do they attempt to carry away wholly the blossoms on which they do alight, but that part which helps their work. And there are many of the poets who are teachers of virtue. What other meaning had Hesiod in those verses of his which are in everybody's mouth? Basil has heard a very competent judge declare that Homer's whole poem is a praise of virtue. But specially he loves to view in this way that passage where he relates the escape of Ulysses naked from a shipwreck. For he represents him as presently gaining such high esteem among the Phæacians that, leaving their luxurious indulgences, they all look up to him and imitate him, nor would any one of them wish better for himself than that he should be Ulysses preserved from shipwreck. For there, said this interpreter of the poet, Homer cries as it were aloud to us: Be virtue your care, which alone swims to land with its shipwrecked possessor, and renders him, when cast ashore, an object of reverence to the prosperous Phæacians.

And Solon gives a good warning to the rich when he says, We will not exchange virtue for wealth; for the one remains ever our own, and the other changes from one man to another. And Theognis says the same. And Prodicus, the Cean sophist, a man to be listened to with great respect, tells (as far as Basil is able to remember his sense, if not his words) how two women came to Hercules, just entering on manhood as you are now; and the two were Vice and Virtue, the one adorned with every art of ornament, and full of pleasant promises, the other lean and poorly dressed, but with a calm and steady eye, offering labours, toils, and dangers by sea and land, and at the end of all deification; which latter Hercules elected to follow. And we may read of Pericles, who sent home with torches, by way of honour, a man who had abused him all the day through; a reward for the lesson of philosophy which he had taught him. And Socrates, when some one struck him in the face and left it all bruised and bleeding, took no other vengeance than to write upon his own forehead, Such a one did this. These things tend the same way as our doctrine that, when stricken on the one cheek, you should turn the other. Good were it for us to imitate such men as Alexander, when he refused to look upon the beauty of Darius' daughter, his captive. But Basil can scarce believe the resemblance of the incident related of Clinias the Pythagorean to Christianity, to be fortuitous. He might have escaped a fine of three talents, but declined to do so, although the oath would not have been a false one; and thus taught, Basil thinks, our principle that oaths are forbidden.

And then he remembers the long and severe trials in self-denial which preceded the contests of the Grecian games, with no greater reward to look forward to than a crown of parsley or wild olive. And he finds among the classic records warning against voluptuous music, and incentive to love only that music which is high and pure, as was that of David. It is told that Pythagoras once recalled a party of revellers to their senses by ordering the flute-players to play in the Doric mode. And with his usual interest in the improvement of music Basil warns young men that the music in vogue in their time is altogether to be avoided.

The ancients knew how to despise riches. How much to be admired is Diogenes, who pronounced himself richer than a king because he had fewer wants! Good was the judgment of Socrates, who declared that he would not admire a rich man until he saw by experience that he knew how to use his wealth. If Phidias and Polycletus had been very proud of the gold and ivory of their statues, they would have been laughed at, since they would have been forgetting their art, which added beauty and value to the gold, and boasting of rich materials not their own; and when we think that a man's virtue is not the best ornament of his life, do we not commit the very same mistake?

The last-quoted sentence is interesting as being one of the very few passages (if, indeed, there be any others) in which Basil shows a perception of art. Though his love for natural beauty was so great; though he had spent so long a time at Athens at a period when, in spite of all its losses, it was still richly furnished with the best art the world has seen; and though, along with other buildings, he erected churches, and is recorded by Gregory Nazianzen and Ephrem Syrus to have devoted attention to their ornament, yet we can furnish little proof from his works that he loved either painting, sculpture, or architecture. Assuredly we can find no sign of a barbarous contempt for art; but the proof of taste is wanting too

Basil kept up to the last his acquaintance with the sophists and rhetoricians, among whom he had received his culture; nor do we ever find him making little of them or of their lore. What we do find is a curious air of trifling in his communications with them and theirs with him. In this intercourse elaborate compliments seem to be considered necessary. Literary vanity is nothing to be ashamed of; is, on the contrary, to be fed with all the admiration it can require. The lack of moral earnestness which existed in the heathen of the day forms the strongest contrast to the intensity of conviction, the diligent detection and reproval of mental faults, the indifference to human praise which we find in Basil's Christian correspondence. Why do you not write, Basil says to Leontius, when it is no trouble to a sophist to write? Nay, if your hand is tired, you need not even write; another will do it for you. You only require your tongue, which, if it be not talking to me, will assuredly be talking to some one of those about. And if no one were present it would be talking to itself. Silent it could never be, since it is the tongue of the sophist and Attic. For me, my constant occupation must plead my excuse for not writing; and a kind of vulgarity of speech from constant use of the vernacular makes me quite unfit for addressing you sophists, who, unless you hear something which you consider worthy of your importance, are indignant. If the correspondence of Libanius with Basil be genuine it is a still more striking example of frivolity. Libanius was with some friends when Basil's letter arrived. He read it over in silence, and then smiling and pleased, he said: "I am beaten." "Beaten?" they asked; "and how; and if you be beaten, why are you not sad?" "I am beaten in beauty of letter-writing. Basil has overcome me; and he is my friend. For that reason I am pleased." By which fiction, Basil sensibly replies, he is treating his correspondent as a father does his child when he pretends to be overcome by him in play.

It is characteristic of Basil's use of the classics that we never find him using the names of heathen divinities in sport, or as a figure of speech. With other Christian writers, not far from his time, it is as common to invoke the Muses as the same apostrophe is, or once was, among us. But whether it was that heathenism had too lately ceased to be formidable, or whether it was because of the serious spirit of the man, we find no such playful use of the names of the vanishing mythology in Basil.

It is probable that he knew no Latin. Certainly we do not find any quotations from Latin authors in his works; and amongst so many Greek it is impossible but that some of the sister tongue would have occurred had the writer been acquainted with them.

CHAPTER XVII
The Bible Scholar

There never was a saint whose spiritual life was more constantly fed and inspired by Scripture than was Basil's. The Bible was his life-long study, and his knowledge of it was thorough. At the end of his life he became, as he himself tells us, very fastidious and chary in the reading of new books, because his strength of body scarce sufficed "for reading the inspired Scripture laboriously, and as it ought to be done."[275] His controversial works display an inexhaustible command of Scripture references, never heaped together for mere effect, but most intelligently used. His *apparatus criticus* was not large, consisting chiefly of Aquila and Symmachus,[276] Theodotion and Origen. It is apparent, from the manner in which he discusses critical points in the Old Testament, that he did not know Hebrew.[277] And his commentary upon the first sixteen chapters of Isaiah (if, indeed, it be genuine) is not one of his best

---

[275] Ep. ccxliv.

[276] Hom. in Ps. xliv. 4.

[277] *See, e.g.* the discussion upon "A Virgin shall conceive." Comment. in Esai., *in loc.*

176

works. It is in a living application of Scripture to man's spiritual needs that he shows his mastery and his love of it, and here he has probably been rarely excelled. The Moralia or Ethics form a code of rules of moral and spiritual life, proved and illustrated by Scripture, which may still be studied with much profit and delight. It draws out for the use of Christians a multitude of lessons from the Bible, with the most delicate beauty and truth, and the completeness of the system of higher morals thus compiled might afford to many a doubter no mean proof of the divine origin of the book which can be thus used.

His belief in the inspiration of Scripture was very strong. All Scripture was given by inspiration of God, that all men according to the nature of their sickness might draw medicine from this common repository.[278] He approves of scrutinizing its very syllables, and a proof from it is final. At the same time, he cannot have believed that the faculties of the human instruments were abolished in inspiration; for he argues that while an evil power laying snares for the soul might well be thought capable of confounding men's intellects, it were impious to allege that this could be done by the Spirit of God.[279] Obscurities in Scripture appear to him to have a use in exercising the powers of the mind analogous to that which the difficulties in procuring the necessaries of life have in the outward life of man.[280] And no writer has ever made a more unreserved assertion of the sufficiency of Scripture than this, "If everything which is not of faith is sin, as the Apostle says, while faith cometh by hearing, and hearing by the Word of God, then

---

[278] In Ps. 1:1.
[279] Prooem. in Es. 5.
[280] Ib. 6.

everything which is outside inspired Scripture, not being of faith, is sin."[281] "Let inspired Scripture be our arbiter, and with whomsoever are found the doctrines which agree with the Divine Words these must be voted by all means to speak truth."[282]

If we ask what the reasoning was upon which Basil founded this strong belief in the inspiration of Scripture we do not find any very clear answer in his writings. It appears there rather as a principle which amidst all the free thinking of the time he might count as admitted and uncontested. But upon recurring to the Philocalia,[283] or selection of passages from the works of Origen which occupied Basil and Gregory in their retreat at Annesi, we perceive that the question of the proofs of inspiration had engaged them very deeply, and that they found in their great master no mean treatment of it.

But though Basil resorted with most of the great minds of the time to the works of Origen as a mine of suggestive thought, he by no means accepted that author's allegorical method of exposition. Basil is one who when water is mentioned takes it to mean water.[284] He is acquainted with the laws of allegory though he has not invented them, but entered in this respect into the labours of others; they will not be content that water should mean water, but something else, and plants and fishes they interpret according to their own notions, and the production of reptiles and cattle they expound in a manner distorted to suit their allegory just as the interpreters of dreams who suit their exposition to their own purpose. "But when I hear of grass, of plants, and

---

[281] Moralia, Reg. lxxx., cap. xxii.
[282] Ep. clxxxix.
[283] *See* Lommatzsch's edition of Origen, vol. xxv.
[284] Hexaem., Hom. iii. 9.

fish, I receive all as it is said." Many, however, will think that Basil is not quite true to his own principles of literalism when, reading in Ps. 28:6, "the beloved" as "the son of the unicorns," he explains the unicorn in its strength and with its one horn to mean our Lord in His nature one with the Father.

But this is almost a singular instance. It is not allegory, but a fair application (however it may pass beyond the direct intention of the original) when he takes occasion from the words *nor sat in the seat of the scornful* to warn his hearers against the danger of watching sin with sympathy or approval, because spending our time in the midst of sin begets a habit of mind which we can scarce shake off, and passes on to give a thoroughly plain-spoken description of the evil sights and words which were to be heard and seen in their own market-place and warning against contact with it. Or when he applies *heaviness may endure for a night, but joy cometh in the morning* to the sorrow of the disciples over their buried Lord, and the consolation which His resurrection brought, or to the sorrows of this whole world in which they who happily have wept over their sin shall be comforted, and when the morning of the judgment comes receive their consolation. "They then who pass, in bewailing their sins, their days in this world which is now in its consummation and declines towards its setting, shall rejoice when that true dawn shall come. For they that sow in tears shall reap in joy."

St. Basil's magnificent encomium on the Psalms is well known, nor could we venture to give it in any other rendering than the stately English of Hooker.

Among the books of the Bible the Gospels were his favourite study, and among these St. John. Every utterance of the evangelists excels in magnificence the other teachings of the Spirit, inasmuch as in the others He spake to us by His servants the prophets, but in these Gospels the Lord addresses us Himself. But he who amongst the evangelist preachers is the trumpet-tongued, uttering things beyond human hearing and the understanding of man, is John, the Son of Thunder.[285] Nor does Basil's high conception of the inspiration of Scripture induce him to think that all parts of it are equally useful. "Neglect not reading, especially in the New Testament, because injury often springs from the reading of the Old, not because the things written were injurious, but because of the weakness of those who receive the injury."[286]

Some specimens of Basil's moral applications of Scripture will show how well he knew his Bible, and with what insight he used it. In the Ethica[287] the rule is laid down, that he who loves others in the manner which Christ approves, must not shrink from sometimes causing them grief; the Scripture proof is found in St. John 16:5, 7, where our Lord says, *because I go away, sorrow hath filled your heart; but it is expedient for you that I go:* and 2 Cor. 7:7, where St. Paul rejoices that his letter made the Corinthians *sorry after a godly sort.* The awful rule of God, that men are punished for sin by being delivered to greater sin, is proved from Rom. 1:28, *because they did not like to retain God in their knowledge, God gave them over unto a reprobate mind;* and 2 Thess. 2:10, 11, *because they received not the love of the truth, God sendeth them strong delusion, that they should believe a lie.*[288] Every time is a fit time for doing what pleases God: for the

---

[285] Hom. xvi.
[286] Ep. xlii. 3.
[287] Mor. Reg. v., cap. 5.
[288] Mor. Reg. xi., cap. 4.

Lord said, *I must work the works of Him that sent Me while it is day* (John 9:4); and St. Paul, *not as in my presence only, but now much more in my absence work out your own salvation* (Phil. 2:12). Yet again, there is a fit time for every duty, and things that do not agree are not to be mingled; for the Lord said, *Can the children of the bridechamber fast while the bridegroom is with them?* and St. Paul, *Stand fast in the liberty wherewith Christ hath made us free* (Gal. 5:1).[289] God's commands must be executed with insatiable longing, always pressing forward, for *blessed are they that do hunger and thirst after righteousness,* and *reaching forth unto the things before, I press toward the mark* (Phil. 3:14).[290] Unnecessary things ought to be done to hinder offence to others; for the Lord paid tribute, though He ought to have been free (St. Matt. 17:24–27). Yet again, the will of God must be done, even at the cost of offence to others; for when the Pharisees were offended at His saying, the Lord said, *Let them alone* (St. Matt. 15:14); and He said, *Except ye eat the flesh of the Son of Man, ye have no life in you;* though many of His disciples went away because of the saying (St. John 6:53, 66); and St. Paul said, *We are a sweet savour of Christ in them that are saved, and in them that perish.*[291] A Christian ought hospitably to receive his brethren, without disturbance and frugally. For, *one of His disciples said, there is a lad here which hath five barley loaves and two small fishes. And Jesus said, Make the men sit down* (John 6:8–10); and *Martha was cumbered about much serving, and said, Carest Thou not that my sister hath left me to serve alone? But Jesus said, Martha, Martha, thou art careful and troubled about many things; but one thing is needful* (St. Luke

---

289 Ib. xiii., cap. 2.
290 Ib. xiv., cap. 1.
291 Mor. Reg. xxxiii., caps. 4, 5.

10:42).[292] As the law forbids evil acts, so the Gospel evil thoughts. For, *I say unto you, Whosoever is angry with his brother without a cause shall be in danger of the judgment* (St. Matt. 5:22); and, *he is not a Jew which is one outwardly* (Rom. 2:28). They shall not attain heaven who fail to show the righteousness of the Gospel to be greater than that of the Law. For, *Except your righteousness shall exceed the righteousness of the Scribes and Pharisees, ye shall in no case enter into the kingdom of heaven* (St. Matt. 5:20); and, *If any other thinketh that he hath confidence in the flesh, I more; but what things were gain to me, those I counted loss for Christ* (Phil. 3:4, 7).[293] We ought to show as great diligence in more important affairs as we do in the minor things of this life. For, *Each one of you on the Sabbath-day looseth his ox or ass; and ought not this woman to be loosed* (St. Luke 13:15)? And, *because this woman troubleth me, I will avenge her; and shall not God avenge His own elect?* And, *No man that warreth entangleth himself with the affairs of this life* (2 Tim. 2:4).[294] There must be no indifference towards sinners; but a Christian ought to be very sad for their case. For, *When He beheld the city, He wept over it* (Luke 19:41). And St. Paul says, *And ye were puffed up, and have not rather grieved that he which hath done this deed might be put away from among you* (1 Cor. 5:2). And again, *Lest when I come again to you, my God should humble me among you, and I should lament many which have sinned* (2 Cor. 12:21).[295]

How, and in what state of mind, ought one to pray? "Our Father which art in heaven, hallowed be Thy name. Thy kingdom come," &c. (St. Matt. 6:9). *Seek first*

---

[292] Ib. xxxviii.
[293] Ib. xliii. i. 3.
[294] Mor. Reg. xlvi. i.
[295] Ib. lii., cap. 1.

the kingdom of God and His righteousness (St. Matt. 6:33).
When ye stand praying, forgive (St. Mark 11:25). *I will,
therefore, that men pray everywhere, lifting up holy hands
without wrath or doubting* (1 Tim. 2:8).[296]

A Christian ought not to care about human praise,
nor claim honour; but rather correct those who are
inclined to render it to him. *Lo, one came running to Him,
and said, Good Master ... and He said, Why callest thou me
good* (St. Matt. 19:16). *I receive not glory from men. How
can ye believe which receive honour one of another?* (St. John
5:41, 44). *Woe unto you, Pharisees, for ye love the chief seats*
(St. Luke 11:43). *Nor did we ever use flattering words, as ye
know, nor a cloak of covetousness, God is witness, neither of
men sought we glory* (1 Thess. 2:5). *Cornelius met him, and
fell down at his feet, and worshipped him. But Peter raised him
up, saying, Arise up, I also am a man* (Acts 10:25). *The
people cried out, saying, It is the voice of a God, not of a man;
and immediately the angel of the Lord smote him* (Acts
12:22).[297]

Workers for Christ are not to be despised for their low
social condition. For, *They said, Whence hath this man this
wisdom, and these mighty works? Is not His mother called
Mary, and His brethren James and Joses, and Simon and
Judas* (St. Matt. 13:54). *I thank Thee, O Father, Lord of
heaven and earth, because Thou hast hid these things from the
wise and prudent, and revealed them unto babes* (St. Matt.
11:25). *Ye see your calling, brethren, how that not many wise
men after the flesh, not many mighty, not many noble, are
callers* (1 Cor. 1:26).[298] Weep not for the dead in Christ.
For, *He turned unto them, and said, Daughters of Jerusalem,
weep not for Me* (St. Luke 23:28). *I would not have you*

---

[296] Ib. lvi., cap. 4.
[297] Mor. Reg. lix., cap. 1.
[298] Ib. lxi., cap. 1.

*ignorant, brethren, concerning them which are asleep, that ye
sorrow not, even as others which have no hope* (1 Thess.
4:13).[299] In things not definitely commanded by
Scripture, we ought to incline to the nobler side. For, *He
that can receive it, let him receive it* (St. Matt. 19:12). *I think
that this is good for the present distress, that it is good for a
man so to be* (1 Cor. 7:26). No one ought to compel
others to that which he does not do himself. For, *Woe
unto you, lawyers, for ye lade men with burdens grievous to be
borne, and ye yourselves touch not the burdens with one of your
fingers* (Luke 11:46).[300] These two last rules, we may
remark, contain the key to Basil's asceticism.

The lxxth Rule of Basil's "Ethica" contains under 37
heads a body of laws for priestly life and work which,
with their Scripture proofs, might be printed with great
profit as a clergyman's pocket companion for the present
day. The standard is very high; but the utmost good
sense and pastoral experience mark the code, and the
Scripture authority is undeniably relevant. The minister
of the Word must not be self-satisfied on account of his
own good life, but remember that his special and
peculiar care is, that those trusted to him may grow
better. For, *Ye are the salt of the earth, but if the salt have lost
his savour wherewith shall it be seasoned* (St. Matt. 5:13)?
and, *I came down from heaven, not to do mine own will, but
the will of the Father which sent Me* (St. John 6:38); and,
*What is our hope, and joy, and crown of rejoicing? are not even
ye* (1 Thess. 2:19)? He must go round all villages and
towns entrusted to him. For, *Jesus went about all Galilee*
(St. Matt. 4:23), and *all the cities and villages* (St. Luke
8:1). He must pray and give thanks for the spiritual

---

[299] Ib. lxvii.
[300] Mor. Reg. lxx., caps. 8, 9.

advancement of his flock. For, *Neither pray I for these
alone, but for them that shall believe on Me through their word.
Father, I will that they whom Thou hast given Me be with Me
where I am* (St. John 17:20–24); and, *I thank thee, O
Father, Lord of heaven and earth, that Thou hast hid these
things from the wise and prudent, and revealed them unto
babes* (St. Luke 10:21); and, *First, I thank my God through
Jesus Christ for you all … God is my witness, that without
ceasing I make mention of you in my prayers* (Rom. 1:8, 9).
*God is my record, how I long after you all in the bowels of
Jesus Christ.* And, *This I pray, that your love may abound yet
more and more* (Phil. 1:8, 9). He must, if he love his Lord,
care for his people with a great love and longing, and
deliver to them the truth, both publicly and privately,
even if need be, to the death. For, *The good shepherd
layeth down His life for His sheep* (St. John 10:11); and,
Simon, son of Jonas, lovest thou Me? feed my sheep (Ib.
21:15); and, *On the first day of the week Paul preached unto
them, ready to depart on the morrow, and continued his speech
until midnight; and when he had broken bread, and eaten, and
talked a great while, even till break of day, so he departed*
(Acts 20:7–11). *I kept back nothing that was profitable unto
you, but have taught you publicly, and from house to house*
(Ib. 20:20). *Remember, brethren, our labour and travail, how
that labouring night and day that we should not be chargeable
to any of you, we preached to you the Gospel of God* (1 Thess.
2:9). He must care for his people, even in earthly things.
For, *I have compassion on the multitude, because they have
been with Me now three days and have nothing to eat* (St.
Matt. 15:32). *A leper came to Him, beseeching Him, and
kneeling down to Him, and saying, Lord, if Thou wilt, Thou
canst make me clean. And He put forth His hand, and touched
him, and said, I will; be thou clean* (St. Mark 1:40). *In those
days there arose a murmuring of the Grecians among the*

Hebrews ... and the Apostles ... said ... Look ye out among you seven men of honest report, whom we may appoint over this business (Acts 6:1–3). He must not intrude his presence where it is unwelcome. For, *The multitude of the Gadarenes prayed Him that He should depart from them; and He entered the ship, and departed.*[301] But the hearers who are instructed in the Scriptures should put to the proof what their teachers say to them, and receive what is agreeable to the Scriptures, rejecting what is contrary to them. For, *If thine eye offend thee, pluck it out* (St. Matt. 18:9); and, *he that entereth not by the door into the sheepfold, but climbeth up some other way, the same is a thief and a robber* (St. John 10:1); and, *they know not the voice of strangers* (Ib. 10:5); and, *though we or an angel from heaven preach any other Gospel unto you than that we have preached unto you, let him be accursed* (Gal. 1:8); and, *Prove all things, hold fast that which is good* (1 Thess. 5:21).

---

[301] Mor. Reg. lxx., caps. 11, 14, 19, 21, 32.

CHAPTER XVIII
The Ascetic

It will probably surprise many persons to be told that the key to St. Basil's asceticism is found in his devoted submission to the authority of Holy Scripture. He is so far from claiming any right to go beyond Scripture that he thinks it necessary to apologise for even using words which are not found in the Bible.[302] Those therefore who would understand him must divest themselves in the first place of that vague association of the Fathers with extra-Scriptural traditions which exists in many minds; and in the next place of that firm persuasion which many good Protestants entertain that nobody ever loved the Bible or understood its value before the Reformation.

The truth, if we would confess it, is that we are now not ruled solely by Scripture, but by our social system more or less restrained by Scripture. The amount of explanation or restraint which people allow the words of Scripture to lay upon social rules varies in some degree with the amount of their religion. But there are scarce

---

[302] De Fide, i.

any among us who do not entertain a very strong presumption that what society or the better portion of society thinks right, is right and that any texts of Scripture which seem to set up some other standard must be otherwise explained. We are not asserting that this is wrong; it is not unreasonable nor derogatory to Scripture to say that God, who is the author of our social life as well as of the Scriptures, intended them to be read in combination with it; though probably most of us do not sufficiently remember how God intends society to be constantly corrected and improved by the power of individual conviction. But right or wrong the fact seems certain that we do read the Bible with such an authoritative comment from society as sometimes draws surprising results from the original words. There are many passages which we should never think of explaining as we do if we came to them without the preconceived determination that they cannot be allowed to contradict the experience of society. The strength of this preconception is testified by its unconsciousness. Men take it so entirely for granted that the explanation of Scripture to which social experience compels them is the only possible one that they are not aware how very differently it would be understood by persons whose social surroundings either left them unbiassed or prejudiced them in a different direction.

Now St. Basil lived in the midst of a social system which could claim no such presumption in favour of its principles. It was not so highly organized as ours, and had not the same power of compelling individuals to obey it even against their will. Neither had it the same right to ask the obedience of good men. It had no such beneficial results to show as those which society amid all its imperfections has produced for us. On the contrary, the social system in his time was so bad that the presumption was in favour of its total reconstruction, and a rule of life modelled upon its lines seemed to men of high aims sure to be wrong. Dr. Newman remarks that when Basil and Gregory resolved to devote themselves to the service of religion "somehow the idea of marrying and taking orders or taking orders and marrying, building or improving their parsonage, and showing forth the charities, the humanities, and the gentilities of a family man, did not suggest itself to their minds. They fancied that they must give up wife, children, property, if they would be perfect." This account of their conceptions is perfectly true; and no doubt the satiric allusion to the self-indulgence of modern Christianity is very well deserved. Still it is mere common sense to remark that we cannot argue from the conduct which is proper under a social system unchristianized and hopeless to that which is proper under one which is at all events partly Christian, and of which there is very great hope. The charities and humanities of a family man may be a very low ideal for a Christian priest; but it can hardly be said to have been rejected by Basil and Gregory. Instances were not before them of such a way of life as an effective and possibly the most effective one. Not that the marriage of the clergy was at all unknown. Even bishops, though the custom was that they should separate from their wives, yet occasionally retained them; and Gregory of Nazianzus is believed to have been born during his father's episcopate.[303] But the current of opinion was decidedly against this ideal of priestly life. Society was

---

[303] The Abbé Montaut in his late essay seems to have proved that Gregory Nazianzen was not born during his father's episcopate: but fails, we think, in proving that he was not born while his father was in holy orders.

so little confident of the rightness of its own constitution that it believed in asceticism. It proved this not only by the constant flow of converts whom it furnished to the ascetic life, not only by the saints whom it chose for special veneration from among ascetics alone, but by the occasional self-mortification which whole masses of people inflicted on themselves who ordinarily lived up to a very low standard indeed. In many places of Basil's sermons we find him in a manner taking for granted that a period of fasting and mortification is to be succeeded by a period of licence well nigh frantic.

Even had the essential unsoundness of society in the decay of the Roman empire been less than it was the change of position which in the fourth century the Church experienced rendered it inevitable that an ascetic movement should take place. While she had been discouraged or persecuted by the world she had in the nature of things consisted of those and (speaking generally) only those who had felt the call to leave the world behind. She was in those times ascetic by the very nature of things. With the conversion of the Emperor the world pressed into her precincts, bringing with it all its careless unconverted ways. What should she do? Should she reduce the standard of holiness which her earlier centuries had maintained, or should she establish an inner sanctuary within which the true successors of primitive Christianity should retreat, leaving the outer courts of the Church to the half converted. This was what she did; and the ascetics of the fourth century are the successors to the protest against the world which the whole Church of earlier ages had made.

St. Basil does not condemn marriage as sinful. To do so is, on the contrary, in his opinion, a deadly error. God has divided the life of man into a twofold course—

marriage namely and celibacy—that he who cannot
endure the yoke of celibacy may marry; on this
condition, however, that he remembers that he will be
required to render holiness and self-restraint, and to
cultivate the likeness to those saints who have lived in
marriage and the care of a family. But the monastic life
appeared to Basil to be beyond all question set forth in
Scripture as the highest. Those passages in the
conversations of our Lord, and in the writings of St.
Paul and St. John, which bid us forsake all that we have;
to sell that we have and give to the poor; which say that
there be some who have lived without marriage for the
kingdom of heaven's sake; that it is good for a man so to
be; that virgin souls follow the Lamb whithersoever He
goeth; that we must not love the world, neither the
things in the world; all these passages, and many more
of like import, which we take in a meaning reduced or
explained, St. Basil took literally, and made a manful
attempt to carry them out. His ascetic writings afford us,
probably, the best instance in history of a serious and
thorough attempt, guided by Scripture alone, to put in
practice the morality which such texts inculcate.

It will be asked what this asceticism practically
meant. It meant, in Basil's case, abstinence from
marriage, as matter of course: but also, one meal a day,
and that never of flesh; the same garments night and
day, and sleep upon a plank. It needs not many words to
show that no Englishman of the present day could live
and work with such an amount of food. The fasts not
only of the religious, but even of the worldly, in those
days seem to show that there must have been something
in the physical constitution of that race of men which
made this kind of mortification easier than to us. But we
must not flatter ourselves that it was because they did

not know what comfort was that they could so well dispense with it. From St. Basil's descriptions of the life of his time, we perceive that large classes of people were living in luxury, quite as great as our own, if three daily meals, elaborately furnished, with plenty of meat and wine, may deserve that description.[304] Nor, again, can we plead that the mildness of the climate required little food. The severity of the winters in Cappadocia seems to have been altogether beyond our experience. It shut them up in their houses, and compelled them to remain there; most of Basil's neighbours so feared the winter that they did not even dare to look out; it lasted very long, and made it almost impossible to receive letters, travelling, in some regions, being impossible.[305] The idea of existence in such a climate upon such fare is certainly unattractive to an Englishman of our day. And yet St. Basil very strongly condemns any extremes of self-torture as Manichean;[306] and professes that the asceticism of Cappadocia is but that of children, in comparison to what exists in Egypt and Palestine.[307]

We must not do him the injustice of supposing that his self-restraint is founded upon any forgetfulness or depreciation of the ordinary virtues of kindliness. Its severity proceeds from the principle that the present world is a time of repentance and remission of sins; the next, a time of reward. But we must be pure of all hatred towards any one; must love our enemies, and lay down life itself for our friends, if occasion should demand it; and must have such love in our heart as God and His

---

[304] Const. Monast., cap. vi.
[305] Epp. xxvii., xlvii., cxxi., clvi.
[306] Reg. brev. tract., Interr. cclviii.
[307] Ep. ccvii.

Christ had to us.[308] As the true ascetic is advanced in the grades of the clergy, he ought to become more and more humble, and when you come to the highest, you ought, in proportion, to think lowly of yourself, fearing the condemnation of the sons of Aaron.[309] The unity of God's law, and the principle that the breach of one commandment is a breach of the whole, seems to have impressed itself very strongly upon Basil's mind.[310] But in things allowed by Scripture, no one is either to judge another, nor to hesitate as regards oneself.[311] The passages of Scripture which forbid us to be brought into bondage meet full recognition in Basil's scheme. But Scripture is to be obeyed to the utmost, and no man is to demand from another that which he does not himself perform.

---

[308] Moralia, caps. ii. and v.
[309] Sermo de renunc. sæc. 10.
[310] Prœm. de jud. Dei, 4, 6, and 8.
[311] Moralia, Reg. liv. lv.

CHAPTER XIX
Monasteries

We have seen how greatly St. Basil was struck by the austerity of the monks and anchorets of Egypt. But however much he might admire the self-denial of the solitary, his practical spirit urged him to a form of asceticism which should not exclude either work or fellowship with others. He chose the life of the cœnobite rather than the anchoret, but ascetic is the word of his especial choice.

Already before his time Eustathius of Sebaste had established monasteries in Cappadocia. But these, if they had no other defects, were at least wanting in the soundness of doctrinal basis which could alone found a genuine religious union. The idea of Basil's monasteries, or asceteries as he calls them, was that of uniting the self-denial of the anchoret with union for prayer and mutual edification. "I have learned," he says, "that a life lived in common with others is more useful for many ends. First, for bodily needs we require each other's aid; in solitary life what we have is useless to any one else, and what we ourselves want cannot be supplied. Besides, the doctrine of the love of Christ does not

permit each of us to regard his own things alone. A
solitary life has one aim alone, that each should serve
his own needs. But this is plainly opposed to the law of
charity which the apostle fulfilled who sought not his
own profit but the profit of many, that they might be
saved. Moreover, it is not easy for one who lives alone
to discover his own faults, since he has no one to
reprove him. Woe unto him that is alone when he
falleth, for he hath none to raise him up. And there are
many commandments which can be easily performed by
many gathered together, but not by one. The visitation
of the sick will hinder a man from receiving guests. And
if all who are called in one hope of their calling are one
body in Christ, have Him for their head, and are
members one of another, how can we be so except
through union in one body by the Holy Spirit. We
cannot rejoice with him that doth rejoice, and weep with
him that weeps, if we are altogether separated from him
by the kind of life we lead. How shall he display
humility who has nobody to place himself below? The
Lord girded Himself and washed His disciples' feet.
Whose feet wilt thou wash; whom wilt thou serve; of
whom wilt thou be last, if thou livest by thyself?[312]

The law requires that there should not be less than ten
to celebrate the Paschal supper; and that number ought
to be increased rather than diminished for those who
desire to lead a spiritual life together. All things were to
be in common: nothing was to belong peculiarly to any
individual, neither clothes nor vessel of any sort; bed,
bed covering, warm clothing, shoes, ought to belong to
him who wants them most, not to any proprietor.[313] It is
told of them that believed that none said that any of the

---

[312] Reg. fus. tract., Interr. vii.
[313] Sermo Ascet. ii.

things which he possessed was his own. And whoever
says that anything is his own makes himself alien from
the Church of God and from the love of the Lord, who
taught us both by word and deed that we ought to lay
down our lives for our friends; and if our lives, then
much more mere external possessions.[314] Even one's
thoughts ought not to be kept to oneself. In whatever
each one finds himself to be deficient, let him propose it
for general examination.[315] Moreover, the law of these
communities does not allow particular friendships or
companionships. For it cannot be but that these should
do injury to the common union.[316]

The first thing to be done by one desirous of
renouncing the evil world is to choose a director for his
future course. He must be experienced in guiding souls
in their way to God; virtuous himself, and showing by
his works the love of God that is in him, and well
instructed in the Holy Scriptures.[317] There is extant a
letter from Basil, sent to the superior of a monastery,
recommending to his care one who has found by
experience that all earthly pleasures come to an end. He
had come to Basil desiring to retire from this miserable
life, and leaving behind the pleasures of the flesh to enter
henceforth on the way that leads to the mansions of
God. Basil had at first deferred the candidate until he
himself should be able to receive him into his new
course of life. But now he prays his correspondent to do
this without him; to train him if indeed he be found
seriously desirous of it; to receive his renunciation of the
world, and have him instructed according to the rules

---

[314] Reg. brev. tract., Interr. lxxxv.
[315] Prœm. in Reg. fus. tract.
[316] Sermo Ascet. 5.
[317] Sermo de renunc. sæc. 2.

and written directions of the holy fathers; and to assign
him one of the brethren at his own choice, who will
instruct him well and make him a sturdy athlete for the
great contest against Satan.[318]

Obedience to the director is to be absolute. You must
use the tongue of your spiritual father as the key which
shall open your mouth to take food, or shall shut it. This
point appears to Basil of the utmost moment He has
known many restored to spiritual health from vicious
habits, but not one from gluttony and secret eating.[319]
Nor is it merely from shameful things that one must
abstain at the counsel of the director, but even from
laudable things.[320] He is to measure the degree of
abstinence, and voluntary self-mortifications beyond
what he assigns are sternly condemned.

Basil is believed to have introduced the practice of
irrevocable vows.[321] Certainly they appear in his
writings. Let those who have promised to the Lord the
maintenance of virginity learn that the virgins who shall
be brought to the King are the virgins that bear company
to the Church and follow her, and do not break the
Church order. And they shall be brought with joy and
gladness; not those who submit to virginity by
compulsion nor those who through grief take up that
holy life, but those who rejoice over it with joy and
gladness.[322] Before the profession of the religious life,
one may embrace whatever form of life he wills within
the bounds of right and law, and may contract marriage;
but when he is bound by his own profession he must

---

[318] Epp. xxiii.
[319] Sermo de renunc. sæc.
[320] Sermo Ascet. ii. 2.
[321] See De Broglie, L'Église et l'Empire, v. 180. *sq.*
[322] Hom. in Ps. xliv. 11.

guard himself for God as a consecrated offering, that he subject not himself to the guilt of sacrilege through contaminating by the service of common life the body which, by his promise, is dedicated to God.[323]

The monk must go as little as may be into public. But before we condemn the rule as over rigid, we must remember the pictures which Basil gives us of the temptations which in those times awaited men in the public ways. "Hast thou left thy cell? thou hast left continency behind, hast fallen in with some seducer who, with her enticements, will draw thee insensibly away. And even if, by the help of God, thou escapest from her net, thou returnest indeed to thy cell, but not the same man; languid and disinclined to any exercise of virtue, and able only after a long time to return to thy proper habits."[324] We find already in Basil a special dress assigned to the ascetic, and the same is to be worn both by day and by night. Those who aim at the same end should strive to resemble one another. Moreover, the habit announces to every one the profession of a religious life which we have made, and they expect from us such conduct as is agreeable to our profession. As then the soldier has his own uniform, and the senator his, from which his dignity is known, so is it but right that the Christian should have something peculiar, even in his dress, for the preservation of that sober gravity recommended by the apostle.

The monk must possess nothing, he must meet no woman, he must drink no wine, he must read canonical books only, and have nothing to do with apocryphal. The minuteness of the rules laid down for him is such as to suggest that they must have been sometimes rather an

---

[323] Sermo Asceticus, 2, *see ante*, p. 68.
[324] Sermo de renunc. sæc. 5.

ideal of perfection than actually maintained in practice.
When you sit, you must not cross your legs, for that is a
sign of an inattentive mind. If you are speaking to any
one who is your inferior, you must not answer him
negligently, as if you despised your brother. This would
be to offer an insult to God.[325]

Sometimes a grave humour is to be discerned in the
rules. You must not say, by way of excuse, "Oh! my
head," or, "Oh! my stomach," calling these obscure
witnesses to a pain which does not exist, and so
infringing the strictness of watching.[326] If any one is
cross on being wakened, what punishment is to be
inflicted on him? In the first place, separation and
deprivation of food. But if he continue insensible, let
him be cut off as a diseased limb.[327] The sister who,
moving her eyes in an offensive manner, gives
annoyance to her neighbour, must be separated for a
week, and the same punishment is assigned to one who
whispers anything against an absent sister with the
object of slander.[328]

The true ascetic uses the driest and least nourishing
food, and eats but once a day.[329] A reading takes place
during meals, which must be listened to with greater
pleasure than that with which we eat and drink.[330] And
Basil concisely states the obligations of his monks when,
in pleading with a public officer for their exemption
from taxes and service, he declares that if they only live
according to their profession, they have neither money
nor bodies to offer, since they have given away the one

---

[325] De renunc. sæc 8.
[326] Ib. 9.
[327] Reg. brev. tract., Interr. xliv.
[328] Epitimia in Canonicas, 3, 16.
[329] Const. Monast., cap. vi.
[330] Reg. brev. tract., Interr. clxxx.

for the use of the poor, and worn out the other with fasting and praying.[331]

Slaves sometimes sought entrance: these were to be sent back to their masters, after the example of St. Paul's treatment of Onesimus. When married persons desire admission, they are to be carefully examined whether they are doing so with the consent of the wife or husband. If not, they are not to be received. But the Apostle's principle that the husband hath not power over his own body is perhaps rather formally than really observed, when the hint is given that many cases have been known in which refractory parties have been through much fasting and prayer induced even through physical necessity to consent to the adoption of the higher life.[332]

The ascetic is warned against a desire to enter the ranks of the clergy, or to rule the brethren.[333] The address of one of Basil's letters gives us an idea of the proportions of the lay and clerical elements in one of his monasteries, which, according to his rule, cannot have numbered less than ten. There are in this one four presbyters and two deacons, together with the rest of the brethren.[334]

There are not to be many brotherhoods in the same village. It is not very likely that more than one person possessing the requisite qualifications as director will be found in one place. Even if this difficulty could be got over, it is found that monasteries in the same village begin by emulation in holiness, and proceed through rivalry in respect of numbers, hospitality, or success in

---

[331] Ep. cclxxxiv.
[332] Reg. fus. tract., Interr. xi., xii.
[333] Const. Monast., ix.
[334] Ep. cclvi.

work, to quarrels and fighting.[335] But brotherhoods reduced to poverty or suffering from sickness are to be heartily and gladly assisted by others, and such assistance ought to be accepted.

With regard to the work on which the brethren are to employ themselves, the general direction is given that it must be such as shall not interfere with the tranquillity of monastic life. It must not involve much negotiation for procuring of materials, nor draw large assemblies together for the purchase of the finished work, nor minister to idle or luxurious fashions. The latter principle is to be borne in mind when weaving or working in leather is adopted. Building, carpentering, brass working, and agriculture are not subject to this objection, but some of these may be too noisy, and apt to separate the brethren; and everything is to be avoided which interferes with the hours of prayer, psalmody, or other duty. On the whole, agriculture is probably the most eligible employment.[336] Religion is never to be made an excuse for neglect of work, for the labourer only is worthy of his hire. Work is useful, not only for keeping the body under, but for the sake of charity, that we may have wherewith to support sick and weak brethren. And it is perfectly possible to pray and to sing at the same time that we work.[337] It is not good that we should travel far abroad to sell the produce of our work. If it be necessary to travel at all for this purpose, a place of sale should be selected where we may meet with pious people. And a considerable number of brethren should go together for the purpose of mutual edification. We must not attend the fairs which are held at places

---

[335] Reg. fus. tract., Interr. xxxv.
[336] Reg. fus. tract., Interr. xxxviii.
[337] Ib. Interr. xxxvii.

sacred to the memory of martyrs. Prayer and remembrance of their holy lives is the only good reason for repairing to such places, not traffic.[338]

The hours of devotion must be carefully observed. That of sunrise, that the first motions of our minds may be consecrated to God; again at the third hour we must call the brethren together for prayer, even though they have scattered to their work, for then we recall to mind the Spirit's descent upon the apostles; and if any for any reason be unable to assemble they should say the office by themselves. At the sixth hour we should pray, after the example of the saints, who say "at evening and morning, and at noonday will I pray." And the 90th Psalm should then be used, that we may be delivered from the pestilence that walketh at the noonday. That the ninth hour is proper for prayer, the example of the Apostles Peter and John, who went up to the temple at that hour, instructs us. And when the day is ended, we should give thanks for its blessings, and confess the faults we have committed in word, deed, or thought during its course. Again, in the commencement of the night we must ask that we be blessed with rest free from sin and free from visions. Paul and Silas, who at midnight prayed and sang praises, and the Psalmist who at midnight rose to give thanks to God, show that hour to be a necessary one for prayer. And, again, before dawn we must rise for prayer according to the verse, "Mine eyes prevent the dawn that I might be occupied in thy words." The diversity and variety of the psalms and prayers at various hours is very useful, since the mind grows torpid under the influence of entire uniformity, and is absent even when it seems present.[339]

---

[338] Ib. Interr. xxxix., xl.

[339] Reg. fus. tract., Interr. xxxvii.

In the convents of women any one who refuses to join heartily in the singing is to be expelled.[340]

It is directed that at the close of every day each one before going to rest should institute a careful self-examination, and should confess his faults to the assembled brethren for the purpose of seeking their prayers.[341] This looks like a system of class-meetings; but it cannot refer to all sins, nor, as we have elsewhere shown, be taken to exclude the practice of private confession; warning is given to be careful to whom we confess our faults; but in the case of the female ascetics it is directed that the superior of the convent be present when the confession is made.[342] The superiors of monasteries are directed to impose penances, not in anger, or as mere punishments of the sin, but so chosen as to tend to the correction of the fault; such as silence for immoderate speech, labour for laziness, separation from the brethren for murmuring, and so forth.[343]

A good deal of educational work seems to have been done by the brotherhoods; though Basil seems to have generally preferred for little boys the ordinary schools to the monastic. Sometimes the children in the latter were orphans and sometimes entrusted by their parents. In the latter case they are to be received in the presence of many witnesses. It is better that no remuneration whatever should be accepted from their friends.[344] They are to be kept separate from the brotherhood under the care of some monk of age and experience. But they are to take part in the devotions held during the day-time.

---

[340] Reg. brev. tract., Interr. cclxxxi.
[341] Sermo Ascet. i. 5.
[342] Reg. brev. tract., Interr. cx.
[343] Reg. fus. tract., Interr. li.
[344] Reg. brev. tract., Interr. ccciv.

They are to be under no pledge to enter the brotherhood until they shall have attained an age to choose for themselves.[345]

With regard to the disposal of money which the relations of a brother may bring for his benefit the rule laid down seems to show that the renunciation of all possessions and the contribution of everything into a common stock was not yet perfectly organized among the brotherhoods; and this may perhaps account for some appearance at various times of the possession of money on the part of Basil himself which has induced some to doubt whether he had personally joined the ascetic society which he organized. It is laid down then in the first place that relations in the world are bound on pain of the judgment of God to bring in any returns of income to which a monk of their family may be entitled. But if these should be used by him in the presence of those poorer brethren who have addicted themselves to the same life it would be to him a source of pride and to them of discouragement. The money should therefore, after the example afforded in the Acts of the Apostles, be laid at the feet of the bishop, provided that he be one competent to administer it.[346]

In exercising the duty of hospitality care is to be taken to avoid ostentation. Some monasteries appear to have been used, when a stranger had to be entertained, to borrow from without costly plate, hangings, and soft couches. This is forbidden. If a stranger from the world arrives he is to be taught by the manner of his entertainment that renunciation of the world is a reality and not a pretence. And should he dislike the lesson the

---

[345] Reg. fus. tract., Interr. xv.
[346] Reg. brev. tract., Interr. clxxxvii.

rule drily observes that he is not likely to trouble his hosts again.[347]

Hospital nurses will approve the penance of a deprivation of benediction imposed upon any of those told off for nursing duties who give the patient any food except what is ordered for him by the superintendent.[348]

Immoderate abstinence is frequently condemned. He does not abstain in the true sense who pleases himself in mortification. Those whom the apostle condemns as displaying a voluntary humility and neglect of the body are Manichæans; not to spare the body is the note of this heresy.

That there must have been falls and failures among Basil's monks our experience of human nature will inform us. Expulsion is to be resorted to without hesitation in the case of the obstinate and contumacious; they must, though with many tears, be cut off like diseased limbs. But a place of repentance is not denied to them. We have among the epistles of Basil two[349] to lapsed monks and one to a fallen sister; from one of which we discover that an outbreak of licentiousness had succeeded to a long period of the extremest asceticism. But in all of them the stern rebukes of Basil are accompanied by equally strong encouragements to repentance.

Basil does not think it possible that Scripture should be profitably studied as a whole by everybody. "There are," he says, "two classes of persons, one that of rulers, and the other whose business is to obey." The former ought to derive from the study of the Bible the rules

---

[347] Reg. fus. tract, Interr. xx.
[348] Pœnæ in mon. delinq. 57.
[349] Epp. xliv., xlv., xlvi.

which are to guide the community. But the rest should remember the words of the Apostle "not to think of themselves more highly than they ought to think," but to be content with the sacred offices and not curiously inquire beyond them. Yet this by no means implies the slightest relaxation of the rule that everything is to be grounded upon Scripture. Who is there so mad as to dare of himself to conceive anything even in thought, needing as he does the blessed Spirit to be guided in the way of truth? he is blind and walks in darkness without the Sun of Righteousness, our Lord Jesus Christ, who enlightens us with His commandment as the sun with rays.